PEOPLES:
Church on the Go

Bernard Palmer

VICTOR BOOKS

a division of SP Publications, Inc.

WHEATON, ILLINOIS 60187

Library of Congress Catalog Card Number: 76-18626
ISBN: 0-88207-656-6

VICTOR BOOKS
A division of SP Publications, Inc.
P.O. Box 1825   Wheaton, Ill. 60187

Contents

Author's Note

If we are to understand The Peoples Church of Toronto, we must learn to know Drs. Oswald J. and Paul Smith, father and son. Peoples was born in the fiery heart of the older Dr. Smith, who was three times rejected as a missionary candidate for reasons of health. Under his strong leadership the purpose of the church was set forth and its roots driven deep.

Dr. Paul Smith, shy and somewhat hesitant about placing himself in a position where he would be living continually in the shadow of his illustrious father, reluctantly assumed command. Under his quiet guidance the program of the church was reshaped to better fit the needs of the present congregation and changing times.

Yet The Peoples Church is still much the same as it was when Dr. O. J. founded it in 1928. There is the same emphasis on world missions and the same incisive devotion to evangelism. The pattern of former years is still evident in the Sunday night program. Yet the unmistakable imprint of the present pastor, Dr. Paul Smith, can be seen in every department of the vast congregation. The Peoples Church is what it is today because God raised up two Drs. Smith with different temperaments and abilities. For that reason you will read much about both men in these pages.

1

The Peoples Church Toronto—Its Origin

Anywhere you look in the rambling buildings that house the Peoples Church, Toronto you will see the mark of austerity. The structures are stark and utilitarian. Nothing more. Rows of Sunday School classrooms are taken over by the Christian Day School during the week, and Founder's Hall becomes a somewhat inadequate gym. On Sunday evening when the main auditorium is too small for the crowds, the Day School's assembly hall becomes an overflow room with closed circuit TV. The offices, including those of Drs. Oswald and Paul Smith, are clustered in an obscure corner, using space that must not have lent itself efficiently to any other purpose. The auditorium, which will seat 2,500 (and is frequently crowded out) is spacious and attractive, but even the most ardent supporter would not be tempted to call it beautiful. It was not intended to be.

The crowded facilities leave the impression that they were built out of necessity, not from a desire to put up a striking edifice conforming to some architect's genius in design. They are as functional as a factory or a college gym, and have the look of both.

Those who know the church and its emphasis on evangelism and foreign missions best are not surprised by the looks of the buildings. Nor are they amazed at the quarter of a million dollars invested in equipment to televise the Sunday morning worship services. The best of equipment helps to more attractively present the Gospel of Jesus to those without Him. The buildings only keep out the cold and rain and sun and provide a place for the congregation to sit. Edifices have never been high on the priority list at Peoples.

A singleness of purpose has guided Dr. Oswald Smith from the day he answered God's call to serve Him, and has controlled the church he founded. Everything that is done is directed by a burning desire to reach the lost for Jesus Christ—at home through an aggressive program of evangelism—abroad by an emphasis on foreign missions that has made The Peoples Church unique among evangelical congregations. Every new program or activity is measured against that purpose and stands or falls on its contribution to it.

The older Bloor Street building that was the church's home from 1934 to 1962 is a beautiful example of Italian architecture. Those who were in the congregation at the time, however, say that even the most pressing of repairs were seldom made.

"Every dollar spent on our building is one we can't use to support missionaries," Dr. Smith would tell the Board of Managers if he felt an explanation was necessary.

The Board, struggling with such problems as falling plaster and sagging doors, may have chafed, but they were never able to divert him from his singleness of purpose. As far as he was concerned, there could be no conflict between the support of foreign missions and any other need. If a missionary lacked funds, the repairs would have to wait.

God Calls Oswald

In the early years of his ministry, Dr. Oswald J. Smith had tramped the dusty streets of northern Canadian villages selling Bibles for the Upper Canada Bible Society, had doors slammed in his face, and had been forced to sleep in barley fields when he was refused shelter. Though his job was selling Bibles, his burden was for the lost. He longed to be a missionary, and had applied as a candidate on three different occasions. Though the doctors kept him physically in Canada because of frail health, his heart was deep in the brush country of Central Africa, the mountains of

Peru, or the bleak steppes of Russia. Wherever God's servants were called to take the glorious news of salvation, he was along in spirit.

The neighbors who farmed near the rural railway station in southern Ontario where Dr. Oswald's father was the telegraph operator did not expect young Oswald to live past his teens. He was pencil-thin and weak as a marsh reed, an easy prey to pneumonia and fainting spells. He was out of school for a period of two years after blacking out and falling during a class.

"Oswald doesn't have many more days on this earth," a minister who was acquainted with the family wrote sadly.

But God had His hand on him. Even while beginning a healing process in the boy's body, He began to deal gently with him, prodding him into asking his mother about forgiveness and talking with his younger brother about trying to be good enough to be worthy of going to heaven when he died. His mother was a Christian, but he understood even from her that salvation had to come through works. He got the idea that in some way he had to be good enough and do enough for God to earn the right to be saved.

Then something happened that shook the entire community. An elderly ditchdigger—an alcoholic named Richardson, complete with the bulbous, pock-marked nose typical of an alcoholic—was reached for Jesus Christ. This wreck of a man had been scorned by everyone because of his inability to keep a job, and for the way he staggered along the road in a blind stupor. Wherever he went he had to close his ears to ridicule.

"I don't know for sure who finally got hold of him," Dr. Smith says, "nor how anyone was able to get through that whisky-saturated fog that clouded his mind to make him understand that God loved him and wanted to give him new life, but old Richardson was gloriously converted and everyone within 25 miles soon knew about it."

The gray-haired ditchdigger was not the type of person one would expect to preach or even lead a Bible study. He hadn't gone to school very much and found it difficult to understand the Scriptures and express himself before a group. But that did not stop him. He was mightily burdened for his neighbors and longed to share his faith with them. He knew firsthand the depths of sin and the anguish that comes with serving Satan.

No one remembers or cares whether he ever considered his own limitations in deciding how he could best serve God. He began to hold meetings in the homes of some of the farmers in the area, moving from one to another each week. Oswald, in his early teens, started going. He was so irresistibly drawn to the meetings he could not stay away. Before long, Richardson had permission from Oswald's father to hold meetings in the waiting room of the railway station. That meant the boy had only to go downstairs to attend. Still, he did not confess his sin and put his trust in Christ.

About the same time, a few believers began to conduct Sunday School at the country schoolhouse nearby, and Oswald and his younger brother, Ernie, attended. It was here that he decided to serve God.

"Any one of you might be a minister someday," their teacher informed the class. She had spoken casually but her remark touched a responsive chord in his heart.

"I doubt that she was even aware of what she had said or that she even remembered it an hour later," Dr. Smith remarked recently. "And I certainly can't understand God's dealing with me. I wasn't even a Christian at the time, but in that moment my future was decided for me. I am convinced it was a crisis point in my life. 'That's what I'm going to do,' I told her. 'I'm going to be a minister!' From that day on I did not waver in my determination. I *knew* God was going to use me in reaching others for Himself."

In 1906, when Oswald was 16, the great evangelist, Dr. R. A. Torrey, came to Toronto for a campaign. Crowds flocked to Massey Hall, the largest auditorium in the city, filling the 3,400 seats in a few minutes. Hundreds milled around outside the building in a futile hope to get inside.

Countless hearts were touched, causing a deep stir in the city. The newspapers followed the campaign closely, even to printing the speaker's messages word for word. Only a serious minded boy—or one God was speaking to—would take the time to look at such accounts. And Oswald read them avidly. At last he convinced his younger brother that they should go to the meeting in the city 100 miles away. It was there on January 28, 1906 that he fully understood what was required of one to become a Christian. Confessing his sin, he received Christ, and asked God to give him new life.

When he went back home at the close of the series of meetings, his mother helped him start a Sunday School for the neighbor's children in the waiting room of the railway station where the former alcoholic had held Bible studies a few years before.

The Long Road to The Peoples Church

"That was the beginning of my service to the Lord," Dr. Smith remembers. "Of course I wasn't ready to be used effectively yet. God was to take me through Toronto Bible College and the Presbyterian seminary in Chicago before leading me back to Toronto to pastor Dale Presbyterian Church."

Revival broke out in the staid group, and on its heels, dissension. There were those—some in high places in the church—who objected to the many prayer meetings and the Gospel hymns. Dr. Smith's singleness of purpose was all too evident in the services for a certain element in the congregation. "Dr. Smith and his soul-saving gang," became their appellation. The situation was resolved by Dr. Smith's resignation.

After two years of serving Christ in various ways, including some time with the Shantymen Christian Association as a lumber-jack preacher on the coast of northern British Columbia, he was led into the Christian and Missionary Alliance. His ministry began to expand until it took him all across the American continent from Vancouver to Florida and the Maritimes to southern California and Europe.

Then he returned to Toronto, where he became the pastor of the Alliance Tabernacle, and the church soon became the city's center of evangelism. Vast crowds filled the Christie Street building night after night, and sometimes as many as 1,000 were turned away from a single service.

"I wasn't entirely aware of it then," Dr. Smith says, "but the philosophy that guided my entire ministry had already taken form. God might call others into differing areas of service, but my call was unmistakeable. He wanted me to be a channel for reaching the lost for Jesus Christ, both at home and abroad. Every activity considered for our church was to be measured against that goal.''

Two years later, Dr. Smith received a unanimous call from the Gospel Tabernacle in New York City to succeed Dr. A. B. Simpson, founder of the Alliance. It was tempting, but he had no peace that God was leading him in that direction, so the call was declined.

In Toronto big things were happening. Revival again came, and twice the tabernacle had to be enlarged to accommodate the crowds. The emphasis on evangelism brought problems, however. The joy of seeing souls reached for Christ was slightly dimmed by the concern of those who were disturbed at the constant effort expended to reach the lost. There was no open opposition, but Smith was offered the position of superintendent of the Alliance for eastern Canada.

In 1927, shortly after he declined the opportunity to move into an administrative position, he accepted a call to The Gospel Tabernacle in Los Angeles. He remained there for a year before resigning to go back to Toronto again. He did not leave California for want of public acceptance. Sunday after Sunday the 2,100-seat auditorium was packed, and at every service people professed Christ as Saviour.

"Even though our ministry on the West Coast was successful,'' he says, "we actually had not been in the States a week when I realized that I had to go back to Ontario. My work there was not finished.

"On our return we decided to organize a new congregation along the lines used in shaping my previous charges. Only this time there would be a significant difference. I would be starting the work myself. There would be no preconceived ideas and methods to fence me in. I rented the Massey Hall Auditorium and preached my first message in what was to become The Peoples Church.''

From the beginning Dr. Smith saw the new group as a somewhat unorthodox organization. He did not want it to be a conventional local congregation with committees and programs and mortgages and power struggles in the choir. Instead his vision for the church was that it would be a missionary and evangelistic center in the heart of the city.

Almost 2,000 people attended the first meeting, and a dozen or more came forward to receive Jesus Christ. Yet Dr. Smith lacked the enthusiasm for the new ministry that he should have had. "I'm afraid I didn't take a great deal of interest in it at first," he confesses today. "My heart was still with The Alliance Tabernacle on Christie Street, which I had helped organize and which, since I left, had been steadily dropping in attendance and membership."

In order to hold evangelistic meetings in cities across the United States, he frequently left others in charge of the fledgling group that was first called the Cosmopolitan Tabernacle, then the Toronto Gospel Tabernacle, and finally, in 1933, The Peoples Church, Toronto. However, it was not until 1932, after his third missionary trip to Europe, that he reached the place where he could love the new work and realize that this was to be his ministry.

"I had been so deeply hurt by what had happened in my first two churches in Toronto," Dr. Smith said, "that I could not bring myself to realize that this new ministry was to be God's will for my life. I was like a mother finally accepting her child after rejecting him for four long years. As I looked out over that packed auditorium midway in our missionary convention, my heart began to burn. This was from God! He had given me the vision and had guided me to this point. He had even given me all of those people who needed to hear about Jesus Christ. In an instant my eyes were open. I could see! And what I saw was love! That was over 40 years ago and the fire of love has been burning a little brighter for me every day."

Growing Pains

Many among the financial supporters of The Peoples Church looked at the crowds that were coming and thought it would be wise to buy or build a larger building, but Dr. Smith steadfastly refused. He was determined the Lord's money was not going to be used to pay interest. The portion God entrusted to them was going to help missionaries and present the Gospel to the lost in the Toronto area, even if they had to meet in a tent.

A Methodist church building on lower Bloor Street was left vacant about this time. The auditorium seated more than 1,600, an ideal size for the burgeoning ministry, and the downtown location made it suitable as an inner city evangelistic center. Dr. Smith rented it and moved his services to that location. Still, he would not consent to buy the property, even though he soon learned that it could be bought for $65,000—a fraction of its true value. They were not going to buy any building until God had first clearly shown them that they should move in that direction. When someone gave him a single check for $10,000 he would take it as a sign that they should buy instead of pay rent. He had been praying for that sign since 1928 when they first rented Massey Hall to launch the series of meetings that were the foundation for the church. Six years later he was still paying rent and still praying.

He mentioned the covenant with God on the radio a number of times, but nothing came of it. Then a Christian businessman and his wife gave him a check for $20,000 to apply on the purchase price. Dr. Smith had his answer. The decision was made to buy the church.

The first Missionary Convention at the Cosmopolitan Tabernacle was held in 1929 following Dr. Smith's second trip to Russia. In three days they were able to raise $10,000 in cash for European missionary work, and a regular feature of the new ministry was established. Today the Missionary Conference—with little change in purpose or emphasis, but with many changes in format, and renamed in recent years—still takes precedence over all other activities. It is the time when the huge missionary offerings that have made The Peoples Church unique are taken.

Dr. Smith brought to his own church the pledge system that was developed by A. B. Simpson for the purpose of supporting missions and missionaries.

"Only the term 'pledge' was too cold and too businesslike to please me," he explains. "I took on the arrangement as a promise I can trust God to help me meet. This is the way we present our program at our conferences. Our faith-promise drive has become the backbone of our missionary giving and seems to take on new importance each year."

In the early days of the church, Dr. Smith was convinced that aggressive evangelism would pack any church. That conviction caused countless problems during his first two charges as a young man just out of seminary, but his difficulties only reinforced his determination to hew closely to the purpose God had challenged him to use as the single goal for his ministry. To carry out that task he sought the most capable speakers and the finest soloists and singing groups available to help attract crowds. The crowds came and souls were saved. These things are a matter of record. But the efforts of The Peoples Church to find talent and subject material that would draw the unchurched have been at the root of much criticism.

"Smith would put an elephant or a two-headed calf or Siamese twins on the platform if he thought it would help fill his auditorium," certain pastors have observed.

"You can't knock it," one minister said frankly. "You've got to admit that their program brings the people the rest of us aren't able to reach. Every Sunday souls are being won for Christ that probably wouldn't be with a less flamboyant approach."

Singleness of Purpose

Early in Dr. Smith's ministry, while he was still attending McCormick Seminary in Chicago and serving a church on Chicago's South Side, he set down the goals he planned to use as guidelines in any church he served. They were simple and direct.

1. *To reach the unsaved for Christ.*
2. *To turn Christians from worldliness to spirituality.*
3. *To make the prayer meeting a live service.*
4. *To build a large, enthusiastic Sunday School.*
5. *To develop a strong missionary church.*
6. *To increase church attendance.*
7. *To put spiritual men in every service.*

Dr. Smith's goals were refined as his experience in the ministry grew, and with one exception, he saw them as parts of his larger goal: to reach the lost for Christ. He was not too interested in the Sunday School during his pastorate at The Peoples Church. His promotion of it was negligible. Attendance in the Sunday School never went above 400 at a time when the preaching services were attracting occasional standing-room crowds of 2,000 and more.

"You have to remember that Dr. Smith did not see this as a family church," according to a staff member. "He was of the old school of tabernacles and evangelistic crusades. The church was deliberately kept a loosely structured organization in those days. The main thrust was the pulpit ministry. From September through December he would have from four to six crusades. There would be a couple in late winter and another four or five in the spring. He was even known to have a campaign in the summer, and that takes courage here in Toronto where everybody flocks to the lakes as soon as school is out. The Sunday School was far down Dr. Smith's list as an effective tool of The Peoples Church."

2

The Torch
Is Passed

Dr. Oswald Smith's Presbyterian background is perceptible in the structure of the governing body of The Peoples Church. Authority for conducting business and looking after the property is vested in the Board of Managers. The elders take care of the spiritual work and the deacons handle the loose offerings.

At this point, however, The Peoples Church departs from accepted Presbyterian practice. The congregation does not elect members of the Board. The Board is self-perpetuating and votes on replacements from a list of acceptable candidates supplied by the senior pastor, who is also the chairman. The 15-man Board does not meet regularly, but gets together at the discretion of the pastor to deal with specific situations. In an average year they will meet 9 or 10 times.

The 240 elders have few direct responsibilities except to counsel at the frequent evangelistic meetings. One of the staff ministers termed the position as largely honorary, a way of recognizing the faithfulness of men in the congregation for years of service and giving.

In 1936 the church formally organized and obtained a government charter as a nonprofit group so title of the property could be held by the church rather than by an individual. There still is not a formal membership, but the church claims as adherents those who attend services and who give regularly as long as they are able.

Dr. Oswald Smith's books have been translated and printed in 119 languages, and more than 5 million copies have been distributed. His 1,200 hymns include some of the best loved of today, such as "There is Joy in Serving Jesus," "The Song of the Soul Set Free," "The Glory of His Presence," and "Then Jesus Came." Some people believe he will be remembered longer for his song writing than for any of his other accomplishments. While that is not easy to accept in view of his stature in the Christian world and the contribution he has made to missions, his hymns have blessed countless thousands, and have had a great ministry.

Choosing a Successor

Few were surprised when the senior pastor, who wanted his son Paul to be his successor, invited him to join the staff as associate pastor. For the older man the choice seemed simple. Who would be more familiar with the work than his son who was brought up in it and knew every phase? Who would be more apt to keep the church moving in the direction he had so prayerfully charted? Who would the people be more likely to accept as senior pastor when he retired?

Dr. Smith prayed long about the matter of naming his successor, and always came up with the same answer. Of all the men he knew, Paul was the one to pastor The Peoples Church. At first he wondered if that was only Oswald Smith talking, trying to convince himself of his son's ability. Like most men, he was pleased with the thought of a son following in his footsteps. This decision, however, could not be made on the basis of personal desire, so he continued to pray about it. And as the months passed, it became increasingly plain that God was guiding. Paul was the man to fill the pulpit at The Peoples Church, Toronto.

For Dr. Paul Smith, the decision that faced him was agonizing. He was not surprised that the opportunity was offered to him, nor was he awed by it. In spite of his shyness he was confident of his own ability to pastor a sizable congregation. He had graduated from seminary with an excellent record and had inherited his father's ability to express himself and command the attention of an audience. He was not frightened by the demands that would be made upon him for administrative responsibilities, and, as his father had said, he knew the inner working of the church as well as anyone.

But there his confidence waned. All his life he had lived under the shadow of a famous name. He was constantly introduced as Dr. Oswald J. Smith's son, and more often than not he was judged by his father's ability. He had always experienced difficulty in deciding whether people were friendly to him because they liked him for himself, or if they respected him for being Dr. Oswald Smith's son.

It was not that he was jealous of his father's many accomplishments. He could honestly say he was proud of his heritage, and his love for his father included a fierce loyalty. In spite of that, however, he was not at all sure he should attempt to serve as senior pastor in the church his father founded. He knew the many pitfalls that would lie ahead.

There were a dozen reasons why accepting the position as senior pastor would not be wise, he decided. His father was a strong personality. It took such an individual to found a church and build it up until it had become the most important evangelical congregation in all of Canada and one of the most effective churches in North America and the world. He ruled the church board with a firm, unwavering hand. Paul knew him as a strong-willed, opinionated, hard-driving individual who was accustomed to walking uncharted roads and to getting his own way. On occasion his Board opposed him, but he was usually so sure God was guiding him that he drove hard to get his programs approved.

Following such a man would be difficult for anyone, but as the son of his father, Paul would have an added set of problems. Everyone would expect him to be a carbon copy of the former pastor. They would be comparing his messages, the way he worked with the Board, and his friendliness, or lack of it, to what his father had done.

But that was not all. He would be serving people who had seen him running around the church as a child. Some, forgetting that the minister's family has the same human frailties as they themselves, would be looking at him critically, wondering how he could hope to fill such an illustrious pulpit. It would be hard for him to gain the respect and confidence of these people.

Then there were those he had grown up with. How could he counsel with them?

Those factors would make the task he had been asked to assume so difficult that he was not sure it could be done. Yet another obstacle seemed even more formidable. His father would be staying in Toronto after he retired. His health was good and he had already indicated he would like to have a small office at the church. He would be there every day, taking an active part in all that was going on.

This, above all else, made the position frightening. But Paul would not have it otherwise, as far as his father's remaining at The Peoples Church and taking an active part was concerned. He knew how much the work meant to him. But having a strong-willed former pastor remaining in the church created a difficult situation. His father could be expected to insist on knowing all that went on in every facet of the ministry. Paul could not conceive of his father keeping quiet should he disagree with the decisions that were made.

And Paul was well aware of the fact that his father would have many things to disagree with if he should accept the mantle of leadership. There were a number of things he felt needed revamping.

"I agreed completely with Father's major thrust," he says, "and still do. The Peoples Church exists solely for the purpose of reaching the lost for Christ, both at home and abroad. But, even if I didn't, I would not tamper with it. I firmly believe that God has blessed this church because of Father's continued emphasis on winning souls through emphasizing evangelism and missions. I would be taking the church out of the center of God's will if we were to shift our attention from that goal."

Yet, Paul differed with his father in some instances as to the best way to implement that goal. For one thing, he was concerned about the lack of emphasis on the Sunday School. His father was not particularly interested in that department and the neglect was apparent. Sunday School limped along, ineffective and half-forgotten. It was obvious that it was conducted for the sake of tradition and not because the senior pastor considered it viable and effective.

The Sunday School was not the only department he would be changing. He had long been disturbed by the fact that little was being done to serve those families who called The Peoples Church their church home. The youth work was comparatively weak and little was being done to provide for the needs of the congregation after they made decisions for Christ. Part of the problem was in the fact that Dr. Smith had never looked upon his work as a "local congregation." Because of that, he didn't feel the normal activities of the average church were needed.

"However," Paul explains, "there had been a change in the type of people we were reaching. It had come about so gradually I was not sure Father was fully aware of it. I had tried to talk with him about it a time or two, but he brushed me aside. His interests were so focused on the major purpose of the church he could not see that the Sunday School or the youth program could be a part of reaching the lost. He saw 'missions and evangelism.' Little else. I was convinced that our program would have to include some of the activities Father brushed aside if we were to reach our families for Jesus Christ.

"There had never been any serious difficulties between Father and me, and I certainly didn't want to see trouble, especially over the church we both loved. So I hesitated to go on the staff."

Accepting the Challenge

Reluctantly, and with many misgivings, in September, 1952 Paul accepted the position of associate pastor. But this time he was firmly convinced that God had called him to that post, though he could not understand why.

During the next six years Dr. Oswald Smith carefully trained his son, teaching him all he could about the church and its people. His purpose was to help Paul develop his own potential as a leader. He did not want, nor intend to create a robot who would make every decision the way he would have. He knew his son well enough to know this would not happen. He wanted Paul to be an instrument of God, not an extension of himself. With this in mind, Dr. Smith set to work, delegating authority, watching to see his son's response, and assigning new areas to him as soon as he felt he was ready.

Even though he was in his sixties and was in good health, Dr. Oswald Smith for a while began to spend more and more time away from Toronto. Paul assumed more and more of the responsibilities until the staff was looking to *him* for guidance and he was practically running the church by the time he took over the pastorate on January 1, 1959.

Still the elder Dr. Smith's retirement was a critical period for the new pastor. Though Dr. Oswald Smith relinquished control of the church, he remained as Minister of Missions, so he was still around the building every day. As Paul knew he would be, he remained avidly interested in everything that went on.

"To be frank," Paul says, "I didn't look forward to the time when Father would step down. I thought he would try to run me and everything that I did. I could see some rough times ahead for both of us.

"But when Father retired on December 31, 1958 at the age of 69, he left the operation of the church completely in my hands. When anyone came to him with a problem, he referred that person to me, though he knew what the answer would be. His attitude was so considerate and so loving he made a transition period that could have been a torture, quite easy to go through. I don't know how hard it was for him but I know he made it quite simple for me.

"I think this was the first time I fully came to appreciate the stature of my father. He had started The Peoples Church and had seen it grow into a mighty force for God. To turn it over to someone else must have been heart-wrenching. Yet he had been in the ministry a long while and knew all the difficulties involved in the transfer of leadership, especially after one man had been pastoring a church for so many years. He saw the situation I was in and did all he could to help me.

"I know there were many times when he was sure I was making the wrong decisions, especially during the first few years. Such occasions would be exceedingly difficult for any man, but not once did he criticize me or come to me in an effort to get me to change my mind. As far as he was concerned I was the pastor of the church and he was willing to accept me as such, faults and all. How I thank God for his gracious, kindly spirit. Few men are able to do what he did in accepting retirement.''

Dr. Oswald Smith, now a trim, erect 86 years old, is proud of the changes his son has made. He looks at the Sunday School with an average attendance of more than 1,800 and realizes that Paul saw a need he had been neglecting. He notes the strong youth work, the rapidly expanding Christian Day School, and knows the church is doing a better job of meeting the goal he originally staked out for it. He looks around the bulging church building on Sunday morning and sees that God was, indeed, leading him when he placed his son in the position of senior pastor.

But then Dr. Smith had never doubted his judgment regarding Paul. Actually he had seldom doubted his judgment in anything. He prayed for guidance. God gave it. How could he doubt?

3

Transitions

When Dr. Paul Smith took over as senior pastor, the changes in the Christian Education Department were immediate. The Sunday School assumed a position of importance and was completely overhauled, with one exception: the Sunday School material was left the same. The same material is still being used today.[1] Attention was given to better classrooms, the teaching staff was upgraded, and attendance was stressed.

"I have always looked on the Sunday School as an effective evangelistic tool," says Dr. Daniel L. Edmundson, current Minister of Christian Education. "But you can't reach people for Christ unless they can be brought in so they have opportunity to hear the Gospel. For that reason we have two Sunday School contests or special promotions each year. They have proved to be very effective."

Enrollment today stands at more than 2,600 and the average attendance is 1,840. Though busing has never played a large part in the growth of the Sunday School at The Peoples Church, several vehicles are used on Sunday to provide transportation for those who have no other way of getting to Sunday School.

The busing program, under the direction of Douglas Betts, who

---

[1]Scripture Press material

25

is in charge of the bus captains and the routes, and Paul Neeson,[2] who keeps the vehicles in shape mechanically, brings in an average of 180 to 200 to Sunday School every week.

"At present," Dr. Edmundson says, "we are at absolute capacity. Every available inch of space has been converted to classrooms."

Though Betts and Neeson work together, each had a different reason for choosing that avenue of service. Betts has long been concerned about the Sunday School, so it was normal that he would first think of that department of the church when considering the way in which he would serve Christ.

Neeson, however, came because he was a mechanic and wanted only to serve the Lord and The Peoples Church in any way they needed him. He had been in the car repair business for himself before becoming a city fireman. When God began to speak to him about giving of his time in addition to his money, he immediately thought about his mechanical ability.

"I didn't know for sure whether they would have any particular need for my services," he says, "but I figured something would need fixing sooner or later around such a big building."

When he indicated to members of the staff that he was available if they needed anything repaired, he had no idea they would be calling on him so soon. A few days later his phone rang. The clutch had gone out on one of the vans used for transporting Day School children to school. That was three years ago. "I think I have been here at the church at least once every day since," he concludes. "I take care of general repairs and maintenance. Cliff Moss, who operates a garage, takes care of the major repairs. He attends The Peoples Church and provides the services of his men without cost."

"Our expense for vehicle repairs is limited to the wholesale cost of the parts," Dr. Edmundson adds.

Doug Betts assumed charge of the bus captains a year and a half ago. He got several youthful volunteers to help him go through the

---

[2]In addition to keeping the buses in good repair and recruiting and directing the bus drivers, Paul Neesen also does much of the technical maintenance around the church. He recently completed the preliminary sketches for a new high school building that will cost almost $800,000.

apartment complexes in a given area, knocking on doors and inviting kids to ride the buses to Sunday School. Once the kids start attending regularly, teams of adults go out to visit the parents, encouraging them to come too.

"We have learned that we have to be very wise in our approach to the parents of the bus kids," Dr. Paul Smith warns. "If we push too hard we can lose them. So, we try to encourage them to start coming themselves without pressing so much that we frighten them away."

"We have an unusual situation," Dr. Edmundson reports, "in that our strongest Sunday School department is the adult department. I have visited few Sunday Schools with that situation. We have an average of 750 to 800 adults every Sunday."

This was not always true. A few years ago the adult classes dropped regular Sunday School material and went to an elective program with the classes being taught by the various department ministers. After a couple of years attendance began to lag.

"We found that 80% of the classes were studying prophecy," Dr. Paul Smith says, "and had been since the elective program was instituted. Now it's fine to study prophecy. Every believer should know what God has to say on the subject, but a preoccupation with any particular subject or doctrine of the Bible is not wise. I am not criticizing the program of electives in the adult department of a Sunday School. All I am saying is that it did not work well for us, and our adult department has been much stronger since it was dropped in favor of regular material."

Probably the most unusual feature of their Sunday School has been the way God has used it to help and strengthen the missionary thrust of The Peoples Church. It was one of the most important departments in the entire church as far as the faith-promise program for missionary giving is concerned. In 1974 $400,000 came in for missions through the Sunday School. In 1975 it was half a million dollars.

Envelopes are passed out to all departments. "Even the beginners are encouraged to make a faith-promise, even if it is only three or five cents each week," Sunday School superintendent Wilfred Wright, who is president of Associated Biscuits of Canada, says.

"We want to teach them to be concerned about missions and missionaries and how to give. During the annual missions conference we have missionary speakers in all of the Sunday School departments and urge everyone to attend the nightly meetings. I've never seen any figures on this, but I have a feeling that many of the young people from The Peoples Church who go out to the various mission fields of the world do so because of the strong missionary emphasis in our Sunday School."

The Sunday School has become an important factor in realizing the purpose of the church—reaching souls for Christ, both at home and around the world.

A Day School

When The Peoples Church was first organized, no one thought there would ever be a Christian day school associated with it. Such a venture seemed so far from the purpose of the group that it was not discussed seriously during the early years.

But Dr. Paul Smith and others became concerned about the influence of the public schools on the children from Christian homes. They saw where the humanistic approach to life, the permissiveness, and lack of discipline were leading, and it disturbed them greatly. Though the subject came up from time to time, it was pushed aside.

"Nevertheless, I had been thinking seriously about instituting it for a long while," Paul says. "One Sunday morning I mentioned it as a long-range goal, along with some of my reasons for wanting to see such a school. It came into the message almost casually. I don't even remember now why I said anything about it. I suppose I thought it might stimulate a little interest and help to let the people get used to the idea, but I had no plans beyond that."

However, a reporter in the audience made notes, and the next day the paper carried the announcement on the front page that The Peoples Church was going to start a Christian day school in the immediate future. Either the reporter missed Dr. Smith's statement that the plans for the day school were some distance into the future, or he chose to ignore it. The other two local papers also carried the story, which increased the exposure.

"Dr. Edmundson was away at the time," Paul says, "but as soon as he got home I called him in. 'We're getting a lot of exposure on this school idea. What do you say we go ahead with our plans?' "

He was as ready as Paul was, only a bit more cautious in his estimate of the amount of time they would need to organize the new school and find qualified Christian teachers. It was already March. "How about gearing ourselves to open classes a year from next September?" Dr. Edmundson asked.

"I think we ought to start this September," replied Paul. "We have momentum now. We might lose it if we wait another year."

Dr. Edmundson could scarcely believe he had heard correctly. September was only six months away and all they had were some Sunday School rooms for classes. They could never get a day school off the ground that fast.

But Paul was adamant. The matter was brought before the Board and passed by an overwhelming majority. Now that the decision was made, he would have started classes the following Monday had that been possible.

There were a number of things that helped The Peoples Church move rapidly in launching their school. The City Board of Education was sympathetic and gave them a great deal of valuable advice and guidance. When the adjoining educational unit was built, the church had followed the provincial specifications for school classrooms. The window space and interior lighting met the public school specifications. The Founders Hall was an older structure that was neither large enough nor high enough, but could serve as a gym for a while.

There was a surplus of teachers at that particular time—something that wasn't true even two years earlier. They had 15 applications from well-qualified Christians for each of the openings on the staff.

While Dr. Edmundson was assembling a competent staff of teachers, he was also ordering equipment and selecting text books. Tuition rates were set and applications were accepted.

"The first thing we knew we had a Christian day school," Dr. Edmundson says. "And it was ready in plenty of time for the September opening. I didn't believe it could be done, but with God all things are possible.''

"There was one thing going for us that made a great deal of difference in the cooperation we were able to get from the public schools,'' Paul recalls, ''though I don't believe we were aware of it at the time. We had never fought the public schools nor criticized them from the pulpit. In fact we had done everything we could to cooperate with them. So when we approached them for guidance we were able to come as friends. I'm sure this made a great deal of difference in the support we got from the Toronto school system.''

Today there are approximately 470 students enrolled. Two-thirds of that number come from outside The Peoples Church, with representatives from 95 different churches. There are two basic requirements for enrollment. Each prospective student is given a battery of tests and must have a normal IQ of 90—or above. In addition he must have an achievement level within five or six months of his grade level.

More Growth

Though the plan was to provide all grades through high school, the first year the school provided classes for those in kindergarten through grade eight. The second year the curriculum was enlarged to include kindergarten through grade nine. The third year they began with junior kindergarten, which takes four-year-olds, and enlarged the high school to include grade 12. Grade 13 will be added in September, 1976.

Tuition pays from 90% to 95% of the total cost, so the subsidization by the church is nominal.

Ontario has one of the highest pay scales for teachers anywhere in North America, and, as the province's largest city, Toronto is among the top paying. The church has never been able to equal the salary the staff could get for a comparable teaching position elsewhere, so each member of the staff remains with them at a considerable personal sacrifice.

"While we're anxious to pay as much as we possibly can," Paul says, "we fall short of equaling the pay offered by the public school system by 10 to 20 percent. Though this isn't done deliberately for any reason other than a lack of funds, it does put us in a good situation. It helps us get, and keep, the most dedicated of teachers. Those who are looking only at the size of their paychecks are not interested in being on our staff."

The school has become so popular, that in 1975 almost 300 applications could not be accepted because of lack of space and instructors.

"I'm not sure what the thinking of the Board is on the subject," says Jeremy Sinnott, principal of the high school, "but I'm convinced that we are eventually going to have to build a high school building[3] if we are to meet the needs of the future."

Others in positions of authority at the church agree with him. Early in 1976, Paul Neeson began working on preliminary sketches for an $800,000 high school building at the request of the Board.

Though parents often come to enroll their children in the day school, Norman Asplund, principal of the elementary school for the past four years, likes to have the kids *want* to attend school there before agreeing to take them. "If they come to us because they want to, they are more willing to accept our guidance and we can be of more help to them," he says.

A couple of students who were in the high school at The Peoples Church for the 1974-75 term did not apply to return the next fall. The day after school started one of them was back, pleading to be admitted.

"You should see the English textbook I would be studying from," she explained. "It's filled with profanity. I decided right then that I'd had all I wanted there. I couldn't imagine what it would be like having to sit in a class of that sort day after day, studying books with that kind of language in them, so I came back."

A week later the other student returned. "I didn't like the attitude of the teachers," she said. "They're so haphazard and uncaring. I want to be in a school where the teachers are concerned about me."

---

[3]Now under construction

"These really aren't isolated cases," the principal says. "We have had that sort of thing happen every year since I first came."

Most of the students in the high school are professing believers, according to Sinnott, but they often will realize, after they have been in the school for a time, that they have never really made a personal commitment of their lives to Jesus Christ, and decide to do so.

One morning at the faculty devotions, a teacher shared a testimony concerning some of her students. At recess one of the girls informed the others that she had been born twice, once in Toronto and once in Toronto. The girl beside her said she had been born once in Ottawa and once in a little country church near the farm where she moved with her parents.

"And so it went," the teacher continued. "Each girl in the circle revealed two birthdays, her physical birth and her spiritual birth. Finally they got to one girl who said, 'I've only been born once.'

"At that moment the whistle blew and they had to go in. The next recess the kids took it up again. The matter ended when the one who was not a believer made her decision for Christ behind the baseball diamond. I guess it's things like that which keep our teaching staff here. The opportunity to touch young lives for Jesus Christ means far more than the size of the paycheck."

The Ranch

Another ministry of The Peoples Church is The Ranch, directed by Bruce Chapman, which serves as a year-round campground for the church. The Ranch came into existence through the vision of one of the members of the congregation.

One day a young man asked to see the pastor. Sitting down beside him he said, "I'd like to start a ranch for the church. I think it would be a good ministry."

The pastor was interested but felt that he didn't have the time to devote to it. "If you can find a place for the ranch, Ken, and will take over the responsibility of organizing and operating it, I'll raise the money."

"Pastor," the young man said, thrusting out his hand impulsively, "you've got yourself a deal."

Ken Elford found a farmer who allowed them to use his property. For the first six years The Ranch operated there.

"It was only a summer program at that time," Ken says. "In the spring when the time came to open the ranch for the season we had to clean up the manure and make things ready. In the fall when we stopped operating, the owner opened the gates and let the cows back in."

At the end of six years The Ranch was so successful the Board felt it was wise to obtain their own property. "It was six or seven years ago that we reached that decision," Dr. Paul Smith explains. "Now we have Bruce Chapman as full-time director of The Ranch program. It continues to grow in size and effectiveness every year."

While figures only tell part of the story, 105 campers made first-time decisions to receive Christ during the 1975 summer season at The Ranch. Thirty-seven others openly admitted that they had drifted far from God and came back to Him. Still others, experiencing a variety of problems, such as loneliness, frustration, and rebellion, were prompted by the Holy Spirit to approach some trusted staff member for counsel.

"Even before the summer session was over we were receiving letters of gratitude from parents," Chapman says. "One mother wrote, 'Thank you for your devotion and for the love that you showed for my son. I would appreciate the prayers of your staff for my son, that he'll always trust in Jesus.' "

A father was even more specific. "There is so much pressure here in the city it is very difficult to direct young people. What God has done for my son this year at The Ranch I know will influence his life and guide him in the years ahead."

A 10-year-old camper expressed much the same thought. "Before I came to The Ranch I didn't really believe in God. But after I heard the Gospel and saw Christ in you and your staff members, it all added up. There's got to be a God! Now I really do believe in God and I am a Christian. I'm going to need Him a lot to help me in my schoolwork. I'm going to start reading my Bible more often so I won't slip away from God at all."

Even the staff members have found The Ranch a help to them spiritually. A girl wrote to Mr. Chapman after the last session, expressing her gratitude for having a chance to work at The Ranch. She said it helped her learn how to live and work with people, an area she felt she needed help in. She also thanked him for giving her responsibilities.

"I usually turn people off when I get tired and out of sorts," she wrote. "But I soon found I couldn't do that at The Ranch. I wouldn't be setting a good example for other staff members or for campers. Thank you for a fantastic summer."

What began as a vague longing in the heart of a young man who loved the outdoors and horses and everything connected with ranching became an effective ministry. The Sunday School, day school, and The Ranch all are guided by the same purpose that has been behind The Peoples Church from the beginning. The guiding force has been a strong desire to reach the uncommitted for Jesus Christ.

"The Ranch is an example of what I believe is one of Dr. Paul Smith's most important attributes," Rev. Keith Whiticar says. "He is able to see the value of the other person's ideas. He doesn't have to give birth to a program to recognize that it has merit. In addition, he has the ability to encourage people to go forward with their plans, pointing out possible problem areas without destroying their desire to go ahead. And he can help without taking over. It is this quality, as much as any other, that has helped The Peoples Church to develop such a diverse program."

4

The Staff

Dr. Paul Smith has gathered his staff from a variety of places. Some have found their way to Toronto from either coast of Canada. Others from distant points in the States. Some, like Verdun Matts, are chosen from within The Peoples Church family.

Now 56, Matts has spent half his lifetime in youth work. He was first introduced to that phase of the Christian ministry by getting involved in Youth for Christ, going through YFC's first leadership training program at Moody Bible Institute in Chicago. Concerned about getting more training, he attended Emmaus Bible College for a while when it was situated in Toronto. While attending college he pastored a church, directed Youth for Christ rallies in Toronto, and ran his own insurance business.

"And I was a married man with a family," he says. "I finally had to admit I couldn't do everything and still maintain my health, so I cut my education short."

When his daughters were teenagers, they began to attend The Peoples Church. And when Matts quit the pastorate, they induced the whole family to start going to church with them. When Matts was asked to accept the position of Minister of Youth, he did so, becoming the only member of the staff who does all of his work on a voluntary basis, receiving no salary. He still has his own insurance agency in addition to his duties at the church.

Matts has been strong on getting the Christian youth at the church involved in some form of outreach. It wasn't long after he took over as Minister of Youth at The Peoples Church that one of the toughest sections of Toronto began to feel the gentle, healing hand of the Saviour.

The Holy Spirit was the guiding force behind the move. Two boys from that section of Toronto got involved in the youth group at the church and received Christ as their Saviour. Their lives had been far from what they should have been, even by secular standards, and when God gave them new lives they became so concerned about their former friends that they decided to do something about it. They tucked their Bibles under their arms and went down to a mall in the area, talking to the kids who hung out in the long corridors. Before long other kids from the group were going along to help them.

It would be wrong to imply that the policeman on the beat could notice the change, or that the schools in the area suddenly became quiet and orderly, but those whose lives have been transformed know what has happened. The families who have seen the startling effect of rebirth are often unable to understand what has happened, but they know their loved ones are very different.

After a time, Matts felt it wise to bring the efforts of the kids under the umbrella of the church so he could help provide direction. The first problem was that of public relations. Groups were not supposed to use the shopping centers and malls for the purpose of contacting people, regardless of the worthiness of their cause. Matts went down to talk to the manager of the sprawling commercial complex.

"Yes," the businessman replied. "I know about the boys and what they're doing. I think it's a good idea. I'd much rather have the kids reading the Bible and talking to each other about Jesus Christ than passing drugs."

Bible Studies
The Bible study attended by the kids from the Fairview section meets in a private home. Most of them are still too antiestablishment to go to a church.

"They'll sit around the living room, cigarettes dangling from their lips, and Bibles open on their laps," Matts said. "If I tried to tell them not to smoke they'd say, 'Listen, old man, hang it on your nose!' "

The Bible study has been particularly effective, however. Eighteen have received Christ in the past few months, including one lad who identified himself as the head drug pusher in his high school. Five or six of the new converts have reached the place where they will come to services at the church. Their thinking is beginning to change somewhat about older people, work habits, responsibility, and society in general. In an effort to motivate them more rapidly into a normal life-style, Matts has asked some of the church's more solidly established young people to attend the Bible studies the Fairview kids go to.

"I figured they know the Scriptures and are well-grounded in Christian living," he said. "Those are the two most important factors in dealing with those who have neither. It has been surprising to see how quickly our Christian kids can relate to the society dropouts despite their differences in background and ideology. While it is really too early to tell for sure what effects the Christian kids will have on the antiestablishment gang, they seem to be successful."

The youth department also has other Bible study groups. There are those just getting under way which were designed to be a part of the follow-up program. Others are for the Christian kids who are part of the church. Those studies are designed to instruct them and strengthen their faith and to challenge them to live separated lives. Mr. and Mrs. Dave Hunt are in charge of those study groups.

"We have more than 100 kids involved in Bible studies on a regular basis," Matts says. "And the number is growing."

Counselors
But Bible studies are only one phase of that department's activities. Basically, Matts and his staff are responsible for the ministry with young people from ages 12 to 25, with some attention given to those between the ages of 25 to 35. There are 100 volunteers

working in the youth ministry, excluding the Sunday School classes which are a part of the Christian Education department.

"We're strong on counselors," Matts says. "We like to have at least one counselor for each ten kids in addition to the leaders and assistant leaders. There has to be someone available to talk with a kid if he feels he's got a problem he needs help with. That's why we have 100 workers in this department and could use a lot more."

Only in the college-age groups do they dispense with counselors. Matts believes any people of that age with problems should probably see one of the staff ministers who is experienced in counseling and is able to handle difficult and complex situations.

At the present time a well-trained college graduate is in charge of training counselors. He does not train them to run a youth group or teach Bible studies. He is charged with teaching them to know kids, become aware of where the problems are, and how to move in on a teenager with difficulties, without letting the young person know he is being singled out for attention.

"It's quite a task," Matts says, "and I don't suppose we are accomplishing all we should. We haven't even been able to find authoritative books on the subject, so we have plugged along with what is available in written material. We're not completely satisfied with the training we're able to give, but we're doing the best we can."

Music Outreach

Other outreach ministries of the youth department are the gospel teams, musical groups, and teachers who are willing to go anywhere they are needed in Greater Toronto. They minister in jails, old people's homes, hospitals, and in some smaller churches' programs.

Young people in the group are as busy as they want to be in this way. There are always places to share Christ, places where there is a need for a speaker, a soloist, or a musical group or a teacher. During a recent summer, young people from The Peoples Church ran most of the Sunday services for a downtown rescue mission church that ministered to the people who lived around it. Groups taught in Sunday school, helped with Vacation Bible School and a few regular church services. The college age musical and instrumental group, The Soul Survivors, trained by David Williams, goes out often to churches in the area.

A number of projects sponsored by the Youth Department of The Peoples Church are tailored to meet the special interests kids may have. There is a promotional committee, a camera club, and a car club designed for those whose hobbies are photography or hot rods.

"A kid who's a shutterbug or a grease monkey is often attracted to the church first by attending a meeting of one of those groups," Matts explains. "There is always a spiritual emphasis in the meetings, so we have people in each club who are knowledgeable in that particular area. A guy or a gal who's interested in photography can really learn something by attending our camera club. The same is true for the car buffs."

Help

Matts is assisted by a man named Bob Knight (better known as "Colonel" because of his flourishing handlebar mustache) who works directly with the kids. "Let's face it," the youth minister says, "At my age (56) I could not get down to the level of the average teenager and have an effective relationship with him. I feel that I have the respect and love of the kids. There are even certain areas in which I have an advantage over Bob because of my age. That does not mean, however, that I could begin to do as well in working closely with them on a day-to-day basis. It takes someone nearer to their ages for that."

Knight works closely with the others on the youth department staff and the kids in planning programs. They are varied enough to excite the most restless without losing sight of the primary goal of the church, to reach unbelievers for Christ.

Bob Knight is one of those individuals who lives some distance from the church and still comes regularly. He drives 35 or 40 miles each time he comes to the church. Often he is there twice or three times between Sundays. According to Matts he is dedicated enough to drive all that distance just to meet with seven or eight kids on a given night. They don't have to be told he loves them. They know by the way he puts himself out in order to be with them. Like Matts, Knight is not a paid member of the staff but helps in the youth department on a voluntary basis.

"Some of the things we do may sound far from the goal or reaching the uncommitted for Jesus Christ," the youth minister points out, "but you have to get kids to your meetings or you'll never have a chance to reach them with the Gospel."

In the fall of 1975 the high school gang had a Sadie Hawkins roller skating party with the girls inviting the boys. On another occasion they had a corn roast at a small acreage Knight owns. They've also gone to a rescue mission to attend a service and furnish the program. On another occasion the group went on an overnight, inviting in special speakers. In their last meeting a young man who was converted from a life of drugs and now spends his life speaking for Christ was asked to share his story with the kids.

"We try to be completely realistic in our approach to the kids of every age," Matts explains. "We realize that Christian kids can, and often do get involved in the most gross sin. It is entirely possible for any of them to be enticed into immorality or drugs or alcohol. With that in mind we try to deal with those problems in language plain enough so there is no doubt as to our meaning."

The Rev. Earl Lackey, pastor of Associated Gospel Church in one of the northwest suburbs of Toronto and who has no connection with The Peoples Church or their staff, attests to the fact that the big church does an excellent job of working with youth.

"The kids they get hold of and keep for any length of time are well grounded in the Word," he says. "And most of those I've had contact with are stalwart in their faith and work in the local church. I'm sure they've had many failures. We all do in working with kids. But I've been greatly encouraged by what I've seen around The Peoples Church."

One of those young men who found Christ as his Saviour through the youth department came to Matts a number of years ago at the age of fifteen because of problems at home. Nobody seemed to understand him and he was certain he didn't understand anyone else in his family.

"They're always on my back about something," he complains.

"I can't get along with them. They aren't even happy with the way I walk across the floor or hold my fork at dinner."

Verdun Matts had a good idea about what he was saying. He knew the boy well and had a feeling that his parents had good reason for feeling the way they did. The lad was a rebel from the time he first began to attend The Peoples Church and remained a rebel until he reached the place where he sought Matts for counseling. If there was any trouble in a group or class he was in, he was sure to be involved. Usually he was the instigator.

He had made a decision for Christ several years before and the youth minister knew it. Now Matts reminded him of that decision and encouraged him to be an example at home by coming back to Jesus Christ, asking forgiveness, and living a consistent Christian life before his parents. Some weeks later his mother came to the church and sought out the Minister of Youth.

"What have you done to my boy?" she demanded. She was caught up by such a wave of emotion that it was impossible for Matts to understand the reason for her visit. He was greatly concerned and steeled himself for a verbal beating.

"What do you mean?" he parried. "What's the trouble?"

"He's an entirely different boy these past few weeks," she said. "The change in him has impressed my husband and me so much we decided I should come down and talk to you to find out what you had done to help him so much."

The people around the church saw the change in the young man, too. He still had the same leadership qualities, only now he used them to honor Christ.

"He would get his guitar and sit in a hallway, strumming it and singing softly," one of the youth staff says. "The first thing we knew he would have a gang of kids around him, listening. And if he decided to talk to them instead of sing, it was still the same. He always had a bunch around him. He's going into the ministry now and his personality attracts people so naturally it is going to be a big help to him."

Often teenagers are responsible for bringing others to Christ. This happened with a 14-year-old, though it was not a typical situation. Mary was not a believer, but she had some problems that brought her to Mr. Matts. He, in turn, asked Dr. George D'Sena, Minister of Counseling, to call on the family. The mother was already a Christian, but Dr. D'Sena brought the father to the place where he acknowledged Jesus Christ as his Saviour.

Strangely enough, the girl is not a believer yet. The kids of the church have been praying for her and are trying to work with her but she has not reached the place where she is willing to give Jesus Christ control of her life.

Selecting Youth Workers

The problem of getting enough youth workers is as difficult for The Peoples Church as it is for a work a tenth its size. In a way it may even be more difficult since so many are needed.

Matts insists upon three qualifications:

First, the individual must be fully dedicated to the Lord. "In a job with kids you've got to throw away the clock," he says. "My phone often rings at 2 o'clock in the morning. Some kid has a problem and wants to spend an hour or more talking it out. If the individual doing the counseling isn't dedicated to God, his irritation at being kept from sleep will show through.

"That's one reason for insisting on dedicated people. For another, we have to be practical. Kids will see through a phony. Only a dedicated guy or gal is able to get through to them."

Second, the person must have some basic ability to relate to kids. "I'm not able to nail that one down with any rules for recognizing the trait we're looking for," he continues. "Sometimes we have to go by our feelings. I'll see a gal, for instance, and for some reason I will sense that she's got what it takes to gain the confidence and respect of the kids to the place where she will be able to work with them.

"With anything as nebulous as this, you have to know that we make plenty of mistakes."

Third, the would-be youth worker must love kids. "This is so obvious," he relates, "you would think anyone would know it, but I believe that more youth workers fail because of a lack of love than for any other single reason.

"Some have the idea that if you choose another young person

you will automatically have someone who loves other kids and relates well with them. That is far from the truth. It takes a genuine, abiding love and concern for anyone to be a youth worker." He paused for a time. "In fact, that's the cornerstone for all Christian work, isn't it?"

The Peoples Church of Toronto

Dr. Oswald J. Smith,Founder

Dr. Paul B. Smith, Pastor

The Rev. B. Keith Whiticar,
Assistant to the Minister

Dr. George W. D'Sena,
Minister of Counseling

Mr. Daniel L. Edmundson,
Minister of Christian Education

Mr. H. Verdun Matts,
Minister of Youth

Mr. David E. Williams,
Minister of Music

Mr. Harold N. Botsford,
Minister of Stewardship

Mr. Lloyd G. Knight,
Business Manager

Platform and choir during
1975 World Missions Conference
The 1975 conference theme is
shown at the top of the platform

Congregation during the
1975 World Missions Conference

The Soul Survivors—
one of the singing groups from the church

1975 World Missions Conference

Televising the Missions Conference

Peoples Church Bible Book House

The Boy's Brigade
at The Peoples Church

Pioneer Girls

The Peoples Christian
School Music Department

54

Mr. Norman P. Asplund,
Principal, The Peoples
Christian Elementary School

Mr. Jeremy Sinnott, Principal,
The Peoples Christian Academy

A Peoples Christian School classroom

The Living Christmas Tree

The Living Cross

The Peoples Ranch

The Peoples Ranch chuck house

The bunk house

Learning to ride at the Ranch

The Bus Ministry

5

The Minister
of Counseling

Madras and Calcutta are oceans away from Toronto. Equally removed is the culture of that land whose roots lie deeply buried in Hinduism, Islam, and oriental philosophy.

India is torn by taboos and castes that set one people above another. Canada is the 20th century melting pot; home for the oppressed and down-trodden, a place where black mingles freely with white, and the oriental finds friends and opportunities. And Toronto is the first stopping place for more than half the new immigrants.

Dr. George D'Sena is one of those who found a new home for his family in the welcoming arms of Canada's most flourishing city. He is an Anglo-Indian of British and Indian parentage. Though brought up in an essentially English culture, educated in English schools, and graduated from medical school and from Talbot Theological Seminary in California, he and his lovely wife realize they were primarily citizens of India.

They had an older son who had remained in the States when Dr. D'Sena and his family returned to their homeland after he completed his theological training. As Dr. D'Sena prayed, the certainty developed in his heart that God was leading them to leave India, their homeland, which they loved so much. For some reason—perhaps because it was where their son was living, but more likely because of the quiet prodding of the Holy Spirit—he began to consider Canada as their next place of service.

Still, he did not make his decision common knowledge. He shared this new determination only with his wife, a former student, the school chancellor, and Bakht Singh, one of India's great Christian leaders.

With some help from friends, the D'Senas arranged to attend a summer conference for Operation Mobilization in Belgium. From there they journeyed on to the United States and finally to Canada.

Several years before, while still in India, Dr. D'Sena had met Dr. Paul Smith and had at that time shared with him the desire to go to Canada one day. The pastor of Peoples Church was sympathetic, but there seemed to be no chance that Dr. D'Sena could ever get on the staff there, so neither of them gave it further thought.

The D'Senas in Toronto

Later, when the D'Senas arrived in Canada, they went to Toronto for a time. While there he was asked to teach a Sunday School class at The Peoples Church for a few weeks. Out of that casual beginning came his appointment as Minister of Counseling.

"Most people think that this means that I am in charge of dealing with those who have family or personal problems," he explains. "But this is not correct. We have a large staff of ministers, and all of us do problem counseling. I am in charge of the counselors who deal with those who wish to make decisions to receive Christ at our evangelistic campaigns or our regular services. I am also in charge of counseling those who write in as a result of our telecasts."

"You must remember the purposes for the existence of Peoples Church," Dr. Paul Smith says. "We are here to bring souls to Jesus Christ. There is a constant evangelistic thrust, even to our regular services. This means we have to have a continuing program of counselor training. Dr. D'Sena not only trains our counselors, but also works closely with me to be sure we have enough adequately trained people in that area to handle the inquirers at any given service."

Dr. D'Sena has a counselor-training class that meets every Sunday evening, except during the summer months. New counselors are taught how to present salvation effectively, how to teach about assurance, temptation, and sin. They learn how to instruct the new believer concerning Bible study and prayer, and about a certain amount of prophecy so the convert can understand some of the basic facts about the Second Coming of Christ.

The first year D'Sena started with 40 or 50 counselors. Later he averaged 25. Last year there were an even dozen. "We now have a list of 80 or 90 men, women, and young people who are willing and qualified to counsel," he explains to those who ask about the program. "For most meetings there are enough trained people in the audience to handle those who profess Christ. They come forward as they see that they are needed. But when we have a big crusade, we contact counselors individually so we know we are going to have enough counselors at a given service."

Literature

Literature plays an important part in the follow-up program at The Peoples Church. The counselors give each newly professing Christian a copy of the Gospel of John, *Safety, Certainty, and Enjoyment, The Morning Watch,* and *How to Read the Bible,* the latter two by Dr. Oswald J. Smith. A form is filled out, noting the person's home address, telephone number, marital status, etc.

It is the counselor's responsibility to keep in touch with the new believer, or see that someone else does so, and get him involved in Sunday School. Sunday School, according to D'Sena, is the best place for the new Christian to get a solid grounding in the Word of God.

A yellow copy of the form the new Christian has filled out with the help of the counselor is given to the superintendent of the particular department that person should be in, or it might be given to the teacher of one of the classes. He gets a class member to visit the new Christian at his home or apartment, take him a copy of *Now That I Believe* by Dr. Bob Cook, and encourage him to read it and also to come to Sunday School.

The Peoples Church used to have special classes for new converts but that was dropped when they discovered the newcomers preferred to go into classes where their friends were. "I don't believe they particularly enjoyed being singled out for special attention the way a class for new believers does. At any rate, such classes were poorly attended so we dropped them," according to D'Sena.

The Minister of Counseling also handles all the correspondence that comes in from the television programs, answering those that have to do with salvation or special problems, and routing to the proper department those letters that concern the music or some other phase of the television ministry. He also is in charge of the Women's Coffee and Bible Study Hour which meets on Thursday mornings. "It may seem strange that I would be involved in such a venture," he explains, "but actually, we get many women at those meetings who are interested in the Word of God but are not connected with the church and seldom attend any of the services."

Visitation

There is relatively little general visitation done by the ministers of The Peoples Church. Dr. D'Sena is responsible for all the hospital visitation, and also sees those who are ill at home. "We have never been too successful with such a program," he says, "and at best, even if we were able to mount a successful plan of visitation we would be in trouble. There simply is no place to put the people if we did get them. Our present facilities are jammed to capacity."

Dr. Paul Smith is characteristically blunt in his appraisal of the church's efforts in visitation.

"I've seen many highly successful programs based on the Kennedy Plan and Campus Crusade's religious survey and Four Spiritual Laws," he says, "but to be completely honest, we've fallen on our faces every time we've tried to organize a visitation program. We have done a great deal of general mass visitation. For at least seven years approximately 150 people went out every Monday night. However, it simply did not work well for us. Now we continue to visit but most of it is done by the Sunday School staff and members—not on the mass basis that has been so successful elsewhere. I have some theories as to why we have been unsuccessful in this area, but they may only be an attempt on my part to rationalize.

"At any rate, we are not a neighborhood church and our program is designed to bring people in, often from a long distance. We do this with personalities who are outstanding, with great musical groups, and with promotion. I have a feeling that we are reaching the people God has for us through these methods, while in other situations He uses visitation to interest those who live within a mile or so of the church."

6

Ministering in Music

It is the Sunday night before Christmas. The Peoples Church has been jammed to capacity since 6:30 and the doors have been shut to keep the crowds to the limit set by the city fire marshal. This is the fifth capacity performance of the Living Christmas Tree this season. The unusual pictures and news stories have appeared in the papers, and two or three additional performances could be packed out, only there isn't time for them during the crowded Christmas season.

The lights are dimmed, the spotlights come on, and 130 voices, accompanied by a 64-member orchestra, blend in heralding the birth of our Saviour and our King. The program opens with the gigantic choir clustered at the foot of the tree with its spectacular lighting in six colors. Greens and reds and blues shimmer up the tree amid the ambers and purples and whites in a scintillating, ever-changing array. The front of the church is blazing with stars.

In the second half of the program the choir takes its place in the tree, with a boy soprano at the peak, his voice as clear and true as a trumpet. Near the close of the performance all the lights are turned out, except for the stars, which are pulsating white and blue. Each choir member flicks a small pencil flashlight on and off as the boy sings "Away in a Manger." As a finale the choir sings "O Holy Night" and "Coronation Bells." "Coronation Bells" is an original production; the music was composed by Dave Williams, Minister of Music at The Peoples Church, and the lyrics were written by Hope Evangeline, Dr. Paul Smith's sister, who is also a poetess of stature. It is a fitting climax to a performance that has become an institution in Toronto; an event that is as much a part of the Christmas scene in that Canadian city as gifts or family dinners.

"Christmas just isn't complete without The Living Christmas Tree," many say who are scarcely interested in church or Christ the rest of the year.

"But if that's all we do, complete your Christmas, we feel we have failed in our purpose," Williams says. "The Christmas tree is designed to present Jesus Christ and the true meaning of the season to those who do not know Him."

Even such a popular program is a part of the overall purpose of the church.

The Music Staff

The Peoples Church draws almost 100 percent of its music staff from among its membership. Williams is one of those who began to attend services when he was in his teens and was later called to take over the music department.

When he first began to play the pump organ at the age of eight or nine in a little country church in northern Ontario, he didn't know there was such a place as The Peoples Church of Toronto or that he was taking the first step on the long road that was to lead him into full-time Christian service in the field of music. All he knew was that they needed someone at the church organ when the woman who had been playing moved away. He wasn't able to play too well, but his mother had taught him the keyboard. That knowledge made him the most qualified person available.

"I would practice all week on one hymn so I could play it on Sunday," he remembers. "The next week I would learn another. That's how I got started."

Williams was raised in a Christian home, so it was not unusual that the family would seek out a church after leaving the small gold mining town and moving to Toronto when he was 13. It was not until two years later, however, that he began to attend The Peoples Church.

At that time he was beginning to get interested in music in a serious way. His mother had taught him the fundamentals of piano at an age when most boys are considered musical if they can sing well enough to make a tune recognizable or can beat a drum without getting too far off the rhythm. His interest had been fanned by his experience on the church pump organ and the move to Toronto gave him the opportunity for advanced training.

He studied with teachers who were associated with the Royal Conservatory of Music in Toronto and later became a student at the conservatory. He took church music at Bob Jones University, had a summer session with Robert Shaw at the San Diego State College in Southern California, and studied at Southwestern Seminary in Fort Worth, Texas. He completed his musical education with a Master's Degree in Composition at the University of Toronto.

After serving as Minister of Music in churches in Fort Wayne, Indiana and Fort Smith, Arkansas, he was invited to take over the music department at The Peoples Church in 1960. Though he was surprised at being offered the opportunity to serve in his own church, others did not find it surprising. Knowing Dr. Paul Smith's preference for selecting staff among those who have had a previous association with the church so they know and ascribe to its policies and purposes, it was obvious that Williams would be given the first opportunity. Music has always played an important part in the outreach of the popular Toronto church and he was well qualified by training and experience to provide the type of musical program a work of their size and scope demands.

Choirs

The Peoples Church has a vigorously active music department with a senior choir of 80 members, a college-age choir half that size, an assortment of singing groups, and a 50-piece orchestra. In addition Williams has selected a small, well-balanced instrumental group from among the best talent available in the larger orchestra to play for the church's televised Sunday morning services.

Building a good choir and keeping it that way is not a simple task, especially in a city like Toronto with its transferred people and constantly shifting population. Recruiting is a problem Williams has to live with. He is always needing new voices. And there are always those who want to sing in one of his choirs.

"We ask those who wish to sing with us to come in and audition," he says. "But ours is not the normal audition in which those who fail to meet certain standards are rejected. If a voice should be hopeless, we would try to suggest another avenue of service—but that rarely happens. Our audition is designed to let us know what the individual can do so we can best know how to use him. I am a strong believer in using those who put their trust in Christ in any avenue of service my department offers.

"Really, we are much more interested in finding out if the person who wants to sing with us knows Christ as his Saviour than we are in learning his musical qualifications. How can a man sing of the glories of our Saviour if he has not experienced them himself?"

It may seem to be a contradiction, but they do not always require a new choir member to be a believer. While they do not want more than two or three non-Christians in the choir at a given time, and never in a position where they would be singing solos or taking a prominent part, Williams has occasionally used a singer who does not know Christ as his Saviour.

"We try to leave ourselves open to the leading of the Holy Spirit in this area," he says. "If I believe singing in the choir may help the person spiritually, we will accept him. This applies to those who play in the orchestra as well."

Williams uses the audition to explain to the new choir member what is to be expected of him. There are rules that are not rigidly enforced but serve as guidelines for the various musical groups. It is insisted that a choir member be at rehearsal on Wednesday night if he is to sing Sunday morning or evening. He is supposed to be at 75% of the practices and appearances of the choir if he is to continue to sing.

"We make some exceptions since we have choir members who are businessmen and have to travel, and there are always those who are ill from time to time," Williams explains. "On the whole, however, we expect good attendance if an individual is going to sing or play with us."

In spite of the size of the church and the fact that the morning services are televised, professional soloists are seldom, if ever, brought in to bolster the choirs. Several male and female professional vocalists who volunteer their services and consider The Peoples Church their church home handle those important functions as a labor of love.

A recent development has been the college-age choir, a group of about 40 young men and women between the ages of 18 and 30, who at present are singing for an occasional Sunday evening service. "The new choir is as fine, in every way, as our morning senior choir," Williams hastens to say. "It is not second rate in any way. This is a trap some churches will fall into. They want to get young people into the habit of attending services on Sunday night, so they use the old dodge of giving them something to do—they create a youth choir.

"That's all right, except that often no one is very serious about it. A director is usually chosen on the basis of his willingness rather than his ability; practices are often haphazard; and a second-rate performance is the result. Actually it hurts, rather than helps, to have such a youth choir. People begin to get the idea that Sunday night is a casual, inferior type of service that nobody really cares about, and attendance begins to drop off.

"I would be the last to say that our musical program is ideal, or that everything we set out to do is accomplished, but we do not err by having a casual attitude toward the college-age choir. For one thing, Pastor Smith would not permit it. Our Sunday evening services have to be a as excellent as it is possible for us to make them in order to attract those who do not know Christ as Saviour. And, I guess my own training would rebel at presenting any group that is shoddily prepared.

"So, we work as hard with our college choir as with the adults, and we have a full orchestra taking part in the evening services, as well. The result has been music that is equal in quality to what we use on Sunday morning. And everyone seems to enjoy it. This is particularly true of the kids in the choir. They like being part of a group that can sing well, and work hard at keeping it that way.''

Group Outreach

The church also has a small group that calls themselves The Soul Survivors. Included are six vocalists, a pianist, guitarist, drummer, bass player, and a sound man. A youthful music major in his senior year at the University of Toronto leads the group. The group presents a program of both contemporary music and old familiar hymns, and has been very popular. They took first place in a television competition in Kingston, Ontario and accept invitations to appear in churches, at Youth For Christ rallies and Gospel coffeehouses within 100 to 150 miles of Toronto. Williams occasionally uses them on the telecast of the morning worship service and once a year they will have an entire evening service made up of music and testimonies.

The Inspirations is another small group that has a wide ministry. This ladies trio, with a pianist who doubles as director, is frequently on the televised service. The group is also popular in the surrounding area and is frequently invited to a number of churches.

There has been a teen choir at The Peoples Church in the past, but at present it is not in operation. It faltered and failed through a series of unfortunate circumstances that often plague churches of all sizes.

''We probably could have kept a rather average teen choir going, but we have always operated on the premise that we are going to provide quality in our musical groups or we will have none at all.''

They have never been able to get a children's choir established, except through the day school. ''The people who attend here are so scattered we can't get enough kids together at a time when they are free to practice,'' Williams says. ''It could be that we have gone at it wrong and would not have a children's choir regardless of our size or the location of our homes in relation to the location of the church, but that is the excuse we use. Probably our emphasis on developing a large, competent orchestra has had much to do with this.''

The day school has provided an opportunity to get a children's choir going by having practice during class periods. It is led by Mrs. Norman Asplund, wife of the elementary school principal and makes appearances both at The Peoples Church and other local churches.

Orchestra

The orchestra is an important part of the music department and has been a means of attracting many youthful musicians to the church. Fifty are considered members, and an average of 45 play at any given service. From among the large orchestra, Williams has selected a small group of the best musicians to use during the morning service.

"We don't do that because we feel the morning service is any more important than the evening service," he says, "but we need the small group for the television program."

Williams interviews all prospective instrumentalists, but will only occasionally ask adults for an audition to find out if they have had experience playing in an orchestra. Few are even interested in having a part in a church orchestra unless they can play well. Often, however, Williams will ask younger musicians to audition, simply to find out whether they have had the experience and training necessary to play the type and quality of music the orchestra would like to use.

On special occasions, others (usually university students) are brought in to give better balance to the orchestra. At Christmas or Easter, when the music is more demanding, they may bring in one or two violas to strengthen that section.

Williams does the orchestration for both instrumental groups. This is a common practice among church music directors since their orchestras are made up of the instruments available. It is not possible to get the sort of balance most commercially orchestrated music is done for. Williams constantly has to reinforce weak spots by rewriting the music to fill in with other instruments.

Williams has written and produced two musicals, one on the life of Peter, the other on the Apostle Paul. Both are written in the style of a Broadway musical with speaking and singing parts. The musicals have been very well received and currently a music publishing house is interested in making them available to other churches.

Occasionally the musical groups will produce a "song sermon" in cooperation with Pastor Paul Smith. He will preach a message of four or five points. When he touches on a truth he wants to emphasize, the choirs will sing one or two songs complete with staging, scenery, and costumes. These productions are not too difficult to stage, according to Williams, and have been very effective.

Over the years Williams has built an organization to help produce the more ambitious programs they put on in the course of a year, such as the musicals, The Living Christmas Tree, and the song sermons. One man is in charge of the lighting, another builds the sets, including the standards for the choir in the huge Christmas tree. One of the women in the congregation who is an artist does the scenery and stage designing. A sound crew handles their particular area of the productions.

"Actually," Williams says, "if it weren't for these people, we would be seriously handicapped in what we could do. I would have neither the time nor the ability to take care of all the details that go into an elaborate presentation. As it is, all I have to do is call the crew together and discuss our needs with them. Then I can forget about those elements of the performance, knowing they will be handled well."

The music department has made a significant contribution to the total effectiveness of the program at The Peoples Church, particularly in the area of presenting Jesus Christ in an attractive manner to the unbeliever.

"It's really a miracle that God got hold of us and that we're attending services here," relates one of the members. "We wanted our kids to have some kind of musical education, but we had never thought about getting it from a church. We weren't at all interested in church and weren't attending anywhere. When we found out that Dave Williams had a junior band for kids, we started to attend. We're a Christian family now. You'll never know how wonderful it is to us to know Jesus Christ and to go to church here."

7

Enlarging the Vision

Dr. Oswald J. Smith was quick to see the value of radio as a means of expanding the outreach and ministry of the newly organized congregation and to capitalize on radio's popularity. From the early days of The Peoples Church the microphone became a familiar sight at the pulpit, carrying the morning worship service all over greater Toronto and to other parts of Canada. It provided a means of touching hearts with the Good News of salvation and advertising the outstanding speakers and vocalists brought in for the succession of evangelistic crusades that have characterized the unusual congregation. Over the years since they first tried the medium, they have produced a variety of studio programs in an effort to find new and exciting ways of captivating the unchurched listeners. As the popularity of the programs increased they added a second and yet a third radio station.

"I'm sure we could have gone much farther in that direction than we have, judging by the popularity of those early programs," Dr. Paul Smith says, "but there were national Gospel radio programs in existence that were doing a fine job. I believe Father felt there was no need for us to compete with them."

There were results. Everyone attests to that, though there are no figures to tell how many were reached for Christ by radio. There are many in the church today who were first introduced to The

Peoples Church through radio. In addition, there were hundreds who were first challenged to give to foreign missions by listening to those early broadcasts.

Several years ago Dr. Paul Smith began to consider television as a tool to help them reach their goal of presenting Christ to a lost world. He remembered when his father had first taken the step to go on radio and how effective it had been. He realized that radio had done an excellent job in the past, but now he was not sure it was the most effective means available for reaching the uncommitted for Jesus Christ. Television was a fast-growing medium, especially with the advent of the color set. Evaluating the habits of his own family and those of his friends, he realized that radio had been largely replaced by television.

"I knew a lot of people still listened to radio," he recalls, "but the more I thought about it the more convinced I became that radio had lost much of the hold it used to have on people. The way I saw it, it had become something to work by. It helps to shove boredom aside on a long drive, or occupy the corner of the mind while a housewife does the dishes or dusts or cleans the silver. A kid in school may use it for company while studying. But I felt we had to have the same rapt attention radio was given when Father first went on the air. We had to get something families would actually sit down and pay attention to."

So they began to consider television.

Paul now recalls how stunned he was when he learned how much such a move would cost. They were paying from $150 to $200 an hour for radio time, and television would cost at least $1,100 an hour for comparable coverage. But that was not all. With radio, someone could stick a mike on the pulpit, manipulate a few controls, and they were in business. Television required a raft of expensive equipment and a number of costly technicians. Production costs were figured at $1,500 per program for just one station.

"I was in a state of shock when I got those figures," he says now. "And the television people I consulted began talking about the amount of equipment that would be necessary. I was afraid to ask how much that would cost."

But the Holy Spirit continued to prod him with the fact that they were losing opportunities that could bring people to Christ. He continued to pray about it and the conviction that they ought to go into television persisted. Finally he got someone to introduce him to the manager of the largest station in Toronto and learned that air-time was available.

"I went to the Board with that information," he said, "and laid my burden before them. It was discussed at length and finally a vote was taken. The Board agreed with me.

"It was an experiment in that we would not have hesitated to pull back had it not come off. On the other hand, we were spending a quarter of a million dollars for cameras, lights, and other equipment. You don't go into a project of that scope unless you're reasonably sure it is what you ought to do."

They could have brought in station-owned equipment in a large truck every Sunday for a rental of $5,000 a week. A year's rent money, however, would have bought and paid for the equipment the church would need. By this time they were sure enough of the Lord's leading into this area to buy their own. From the beginning, Dr. Paul Smith followed his father's example in resisting the temptation to save money by taking shortcuts in either the quality or amount of equipment or professional help. As a result they have three fine cameras and the best sound equipment, lights, and console it is possible to buy. They have everything needed to produce a high-quality program in color.

"We have the most important message in the world," he says, "and a mandate from our God to proclaim it. We should have the finest of equipment to produce and transmit that message."

A full crew of professionals comes in every Sunday morning. They do ont operate the camera with volunteers, something many churches with televised services do in order to save money. Fifteen or twenty people who are professionally trained to operate the equipment film the program. A professional producer runs the monitor and selects the camera angles with the most effective pictures. The result is a program as professionally done as anything else that originates locally.

"We feel that the $1,500 or $1,600 it costs us for the services of these people each Sunday is justified by the increased quality of the program," Paul says.

They had not been televising the morning service long when they discovered that something had to be done to sharpen the service and make it more attractive to the television audience. The first question the cameramen had was about the freedom they would be given to move around the front of the church during the service. They realized some might find it distracting. Yet if they were to do a good job they had to be able to change their camera angles.

"We talked with other pastors who have televised services," Paul says. "Most of them seemed afraid to allow the cameras to move at all. Their audiences view the service like individuals sitting in the center section, half way back. I could see that would make for a dull, stereotyped presentation, and we couldn't have that. Not at fifty dollars a minute."

It was the same with wasted time. As he went over their morning service analytically, he was disturbed by the amount of time actually wasted. There were delays in getting special numbers to the microphone, delays between songs the congregation sang, delays in the announcements, and delays in taking up the offerings.

"In fact, our entire service was rather casually run," he recalls. "That might be all right if it were possible to run overtime for 10 or 15 munutes, but when we were paying $50 a munute for television time and had an absolute cut-off time, we had no choice. Our service had to be sharpened. If we didn't do that we could find the speaker being cut off in midsentence, taking the heart out of his message and rendering it ineffective. We couldn't have that and waste all the money we were spending for television."

So they had to go over the entire morning service, ruthlessly paring out any wasted moments so it would move along smoothly and allow the speaker time for his message. The result was a service that even their own people found more challenging.

Lights were another factor Paul thought would be distracting. They weren't, however. After a Sunday or two, few people seemed to notice the lights, the cameras, or even the monitor. They became accepted as part of the service much in the same way the choir and organist and orchestra were accepted.

"The only people the lights bother are those on the platform," he says. "One of the things I miss the most on Sunday morning since we have been on television is the eye contact with the people when I am preaching. The lights are so bright it isn't possible to see the audience well.

"If you've ever done any speaking you know the look of interest in the eyes of the people and their reaction to what you are saying are important factors in the effectiveness of the message. I really miss that."

But the local television audience of 55 to 60 thousand and the other outlets in rural Ontario which double the viewing audience are worth any minor irritations. The amount of unsolicited gifts to help pay for television time has been surprising.

"In fact I am convinced," Paul Smith says, "that any church that can get the equipment and finance a telecast for 18 months will find it self-supporting at the end of that time."

TV Response

"We have been pleased by many things that have happened to show us God was leading us when we established our television outreach in 1972," the pastor says. "But I've been absolutely astonished by the spiritual response.

"It's a common thing to have people come to see me or one of our staff and tell us they have found Christ as Saviour through our television program. And we have had so much mail from those wanting spiritual guidance of one kind or another, we have had to ask Dr. D'Sena to take the responsibility for answering it."

Quite a few letters concern prayer requests. "I've been praying for my husband for years," a woman wrote. "Please join me in asking God to work in his heart and save him."

Some write about illnesses of their own or their loved ones. Others are lonely. Some have been so buffeted by circumstances and self-pity they are beginning to doubt God's love for them. Many will write 15 or 20 times, sharing their joys and heartaches and asking about some theological questions that have been bothering them.

"We read all the letters carefully," Dr. D'Sena says. "Those that require it are answered personally. The others are sent a mimeo-graphed letter thanking them for writing and asking them to pray for us and the television ministry. There is a second mimeographed letter for those who write more than once. We change this letter every couple of months or so.

"I usually include a Scripture reference or two in each letter," D'Sena explains. "After all, I feel my real ministry is through the Word of God."

Occasionally a letter will come in from someone who has been close to God for years, but at the time they found help from the telecast they were going through a difficult period. A pastor out in the province wrote Dr. D'Sena describing his discouragement be-cause of a serious heart condition.

He had just been in the hospital where a team of doctors had examined him, decided that his condition was inoperable, and sent him home. Unable to go to church for a time, he began to watch the telecast from The Peoples Church and found the help and strength he needed.

"Ever since then," he wrote, "the Lord has heard my prayers and those of His people. I am now able to go for walks and to drive a little. Last Lord's Day I was asked to say the benediction at our local church. I was apprehensive about it. (Imagine a man who's preached several thousand sermons being nervous about asking the benediction.) By the grace of God, the Holy Spirit gave me the words of praise I needed. I want to thank you for what your telecast has meant to me."

A subsequent letter related that he believed the Lord was heal-ing him and might once more use him in the ministry. There was purpose and joy in his heart again!

Then there are those who write to tell how God has changed their lives. Those letters, of course, are the ones that mean so much to everyone who has anything to do with the televising of the services.

"Not long ago we got a letter from a woman whose brother had been her concern for more than 17 years," Dr. D'Sena says. She had gone on to tell that her husband had been praying with her all that time for her brother without visible results. He was so hardened he would have nothing to do with the Gospel. They had long since given up talking to him about Jesus Christ or even asking him to go to church. He got so angry and stormed so much about anything they said about Christ that they began to doubt whether God would ever work in his life.

Then he came to their home one Sunday morning when the television program from The Peoples Church was on. For some reason he sat down and listened. At the close of the service he confessed his sin and gave his heart to Jesus Christ.

"Her letter must have sung all the way from her home to Toronto and our church," Dr. D'Sena says. "I don't think I've ever received a letter that was so happy."

Though the church started with one television station in Toronto, the telecast has been so successful they have added four other stations. For a brief period they were on a station in the United States, but dropped it when the contract ran out.

"We prayed about it," Paul Smith explains, "and decided we had not been called to establish a broad television ministry. We may go into it again at some time in the future. I would not rule that out. But I honestly doubt that we will secure time on any other stations. At least we won't until there is some definite assurance that God is leading us in that direction."

When The Peoples Church was first organized, Dr. Oswald Smith established a single purpose for it: presenting Jesus Christ to those who do not know Him. Television has become one of the church's most successful means of reaching the lost, except for the evangelistic crusades that have been sponsored over the years and the emphasis on evangelism in the Sunday evening services.

"That is why we feel our telecast is so important to our ministry," Paul says. "It helps us reach souls for Jesus Christ, and that is what Father saw for our church from the very beginning."

8

Reaching
the Unsaved

From the very beginning, when the church was meeting in a downtown Toronto auditorium, even before acquiring the old Methodist church building on Bloor Street, it was an unusual organization. Dr. Oswald Smith did not see his new work as a local congregation serving the spiritual needs of the Christian family, as important as that is. Nor was that what he wanted it to be. He was interested only in reaching the uncommitted for Jesus Christ.

"Father didn't believe God had called him to use a broad net," Paul explains, "scattering his time and abilities over the entire range of human needs. He wanted to be used as a fish hook, and the more attractively baited the better, to bring in the lost souls to Christ.

"Father always said that he saw The Peoples Church as an evangelistic center for Toronto. Yes, and for that entire section of Canada as well. That was the reason he could see little need for us to have committees and organizations such as the Women's Missionary Society, the Sunday School, and the youth group. Let others take care of those needs. His field was a nation—a world—dying without Jesus Christ. It was up to him to do what he could to reverse that rush to hell."

In the early days of his ministry Dr. Smith was so burdened for Toronto he tied one evangelistic campaign to the heels of another,

hammering at the theme that Jesus saves. He was constantly looking for new voices, new musical talent—anyone who would attract
the world enough to bring people out to the services. All the outstanding evangelists of that era held meetings at The Peoples
Church at one time or another. There were Gypsy Smith, Dr.
Harry Ironside, and a host of others.

A few well-meaning Christian friends tried to get Dr. Smith to
do more to build up his own work. It was fine to win people for
Christ, they told him, but he was reaching out all over Toronto, the
suburbs, and beyond with his aggressive, widely advertised campaigns. When people from a distance received Christ they didn't
consider his church but went back to join congregations nearer to
their homes.

"It's really not doing you any good to expend all this effort,"
they told him. "Why don't you concentrate on those who live in
this immediate area so they can join The Peoples Church and help
to make it strong?"

But he paid no attention to them. "I couldn't believe God was
concerned about building a strong church for us at the expense of
His Kingdom," he says. So the special meetings continued, in summer, fall, winter, and spring. They are not held as often under
Paul's ministry as they were in his father's day as senior pastor, but
they still play an important part in the total ministry of the
church.

"It was not unusual for us to have 12 or 15 evangelistic services
a year," Dr. Smith remembers fondly, "and souls were constantly
being saved. You should have seen how people flocked to the altar
night after night."

It still didn't disturb him to see a majority of the converts go on
to other churches. "I don't blame them," he said frankly when the
situation was again called to his attention. "We aren't set up to
meet their needs the way other churches are. God has called us to
evangelize. He has others to feed the sheep."

Changes, particularly after his son became the senior pastor,
made the church more like other congregations in areas such as the
Sunday School and the youth and women's work, but one factor
has remained untouched. Evangelism is still stressed as much now

as it was in the beginning. It is still the primary purpose of the church.

And The Peoples Church meets that purpose as effectively today as it did 30 years ago. An average of 1,000 or more make decisions for Christ each year as a result of the evangelization efforts.

Follow-Up

The fact that half or more of the converts eventually go elsewhere to church is sometimes cited as proof that little care is given to follow up after a person has made a profession of faith.

"But that is not true," the pastor of another congregation in the area says. "I'm well enough acquainted with the church to know that they have an excellent follow-up program and do an excellent job of bringing new converts to Christian maturity. And that is particularly true of young people. I thank God for The Peoples Church."

A young father attending The Peoples Church agrees with that pastor. "I will have been saved a year in less than a month. It happened when Bob Harrington was here. They got us into Sunday School after I became a Christian. It wasn't long until I was placed in charge of Junior Church on Sunday morning. And my wife and I attend three different Bible studies. I tell you, Christ has changed our whole lives! Both my wife and I love Him and want to serve Him as best we can."

"I started coming to The Peoples Church first when it was on Christie Street," an 84-year-old woman relates. "I heard the Gospel from the pulpit often enough, but I was reading a book by Dr. Smith when I saw my need of a Saviour and confessed my sin and put my trust in Him. And you know what? My nephew came forward this morning. I got so excited I thought I was going to jump right out of the pew!"

"I was saved two years ago in a Sunday School class taught by Rev. Keith Whiticar," a young man says. "I look forward to coming here to Sunday School and church every Sunday."

"I received Christ two years ago on a Sunday morning when Dr. Paul Smith was preaching," a teenaged girl says.

A handsome black from Jamaica told that he had become a believer 12 years before under the preaching of Dr. Paul Smith. "I
am a member of the board of elders now. I also am an usher and
do counseling."

A 22-year-old girl relates that she had been converted at the
age of eight at The Peoples Church when Dr. Paul Smith was
preaching. Now she is working with Campus Crusade for Christ
at the University of Saskatchewan in Saskatoon.

There is ample proof around the halls and in the foyer of The
Peoples Church that follow-up on those who make professions
of faith is not neglected, and that many, many of those decisions
for Christ are genuine.

Crusades—They Work

Strangly enough, the results at The Peoples Church are accomplished by using methods many so-called experts in the field de-
scribe as being old-fashioned and ineffective. The Peoples Church
does not emphasize home Bible studies. They have no program
of visitation as many churches do, nor is much done to train their
people in sharing Christ with their neighbors. The emphasis is on
the "big meeting" using big-name evangelists and musical talent
to attract the unchurched to the services. All across America and
Canada others have given up on crusades as a waste of time. The
pastors of The Peoples Church do not argue with those who have
soured on evangelism. All they have to say is that for them, it
works.

"I have a feeling that such campaigns will work anywhere,"
Paul Smith says, "if the right man is called in and the meetings
are properly planned with the community and its needs in mind.
I don't believe there is anything so peculiar about Toronto as to
make it unique to this area. Anything that will be successful here
ought to work in other places if it's properly done."

No one will deny that The Peoples Church presents a particularly vigorous and unusual brand of evangelism. They have offered
the great, the near-great, and the obscure in the field of evangelism
through the years. Before the world even knew a talented young
Billy Graham existed he was holding a campaign in Dr. Oswald

Smith's church. Nicky Cruz, Warren Wiersbe, and Bob Harrington have been there, as well as J. Vernon McGee and Barry Moore.

Knowing that music has a significant appeal to vast numbers of people of all ages, Paul has been careful to get the finest vocalists and instrumentalists available. Go into any Christian bookstore and thumb through the record albums. The names will sound as though you are reading from the list of those who have appeared at The Peoples Church. Most of the more popular soloists and singing groups have been at the big church in Toronto. Dale Evans, Ed Lyman, Richard and Patti Roberts, Bev Shea, The Imperials, Living Sound, and Dave Boyer—all have lent their talents and reputations to evangelistic services, helping to bring a crowd to hear the Gospel of Jesus Christ.

"One of the reasons The Peoples Church attracts so many outsiders," Rev. Keith Whiticar says, "is that those Paul brings in are the very best. The average person may, or may not, have heard of a certain individual or group, but that doesn't matter to most. They know from experience that they will be hearing someone of outstanding ability."

Unorthodoxy—It Works
But another quality Paul adds to the program of The Peoples Church is more difficult to assess. He seems to know instinctively what to say and how to say it to get the maximum publicity. As a result the newspapers cover the services at The Peoples Church with some regularity.

They are looking for statements such as the one he made criticizing the premier for his playboy tendencies, or the comment that according to the Old Testament homosexuals should be executed. Or they may be expecting to see him put a jukebox on the platform as he did on one occasion to illustrate a point in a sermon.

"I don't believe he has done those things just to get publicity," one of the staff says. "And I'm sure that his remarks reflected what he actually believed, but such incidents happen less frequently now as Paul gets older. However, he is a colorful individual and that makes for good newspaper copy."

And good copy makes good coverage and greater publicity for

what is going on at the church. A friend of the controversial pastor discussed the matter in more detail.

"Not all the P.T. Barnums are in the circus business these days," he said. "And I mean that as a compliment, not to belittle Paul. If he had gone into publicity or advertising instead of preaching the Gospel, he'd be one of the greatest hucksters Canada has ever seen. He has a sixth sense when it comes to assessing the public mind and knowing what will bring out the crowds. And he has the daring to do those things once he's thought of them."

Paul Smith does not admit that this evaluation of himself is correct, but he does acknowledge that much of the reputation of The Peoples Church for colorful programming has been earned. They have used modern methods of advertising and publicity to bring unbelievers out to the meetings.

"And why not use the methods the world has found effective?" he asks. "That's one thing I learned from Father. In the early days of his ministry he discovered that unusual means had to be used if he was going to get those he wanted to reach for Christ to attend the services. They resisted ordinary meetings then, even as they do today.

"I've been criticized by some who say I'd have an elephant on the platform if doing so would bring out a crowd. We haven't done that yet, though I did try to get a horse on the platform years ago. I didn't succeed because he got temperamental and wouldn't cooperate.

"Now, I don't happen to believe that an elephant would bring anyone to church, except perhaps a peanut vender, but let's use this as an example to explain my philosophy of special events and unusual people to get the unsaved out to evangelistic meetings.

"It would be nice if we could have a quiet, dignified Sunday night service that would attract the lost. They tell me that was possible 50 years ago. There was so little for people to do in much of the country that anything a bit out of the ordinary was enough to attract a good crowd and keep them coming back. It wasn't necessary to go much farther afield than to get a violinist who lived down the block, or a few ladies in the church who could sing.

"Let's look at the situation today. We are competing with the automobile that has the ability to carry masses of people out of the city, keeping them from services. That is a competing force the church has never faced before. There are theaters, concerts, fine restaurants, and sports to attract the unbeliever. And there is television. From a standpoint of excellence of musicians, actors, costuming, and special effects, it offers the world's finest right in the living room.

"The hockey fan can watch the Maple Leafs or the Canadiens without moving outside his home. The football enthusiast has his pick of games played all across America and Canada. During the long season he can watch sports on TV until he is numb, if he wishes. The man who cares nothing for Christ and has never seriously considered his own soul isn't likely to get too enthused about hearing me preach on the third chapter of John.

"But we don't put anything on the platform to attract attention to ourselves or to entertain. We do it to pique the interest of the man who can make the choice of coming to church or remain seated in front of his television screen with a glass of beer in his hand. A man like that has to be offered something out of the ordinary or he's going to stay right where he is.

"Christ went out where the people were. He ate with publicans and sinners. All for one purpose. So he might have an opportunity to touch their hearts. I don't mean to be critical of other churches, but take a look at the Sunday evening crowd in the average evangelical congregation. One glance will tell you that the unbelievers are absent. In fact you will probably begin to wonder what has happened to the Christians.

"I'd like to be able to put on a decorous, proper Sunday evening service that would satisfy everyone and not attract criticism. Only that sort of service wouldn't attract the lost, either. It seems to take an elephant on the platform, or something else equally unusual, to get people to come out." His eyes narrowed. "And don't forget. That is the reason The Peoples Church exists. To win souls for Jesus Christ.

"I would be telling you an untruth if I said the criticism doesn't hurt. I'm no different from anyone else when it comes to wanting to be liked. And it disturbs me, personally, when I hear someone say I'll do anything to get a crowd or a story about The Peoples Church in the paper. But I am more concerned about following the leading of the Lord than I am in being liked. In this I have no doubts, whatever. God guided Father into exactly the type of ministry He wanted to have. And he has guided me to perpetuate it.

"And every time a person comes to the altar in response to the invitation to confess his sin and receive Christ I feel that both Father and I are vindicated for the course we have taken at The Peoples Church."

9

Missions

Ask the average Christian anywhere in the United States or Canada what he thinks of when someone mentions The Peoples Church, Toronto and the answer will come quickly. "Missions."

And with good reason. God has used Dr. Oswald Smith's thwarted desire to serve Him on the foreign mission field as the goad that has built the emphasis on missions at the church he founded. Its slogan is the same as it has always been. "The Church That Puts World Missions First."

Starting with five Canadian missionaries, the work has grown until the Peoples Church is now sharing substantially in the support of 375 Canadians going out under a large variety of faith missions to places of service around the world. No one has thought to add up the total number of missionaries who have gone out from the church, but at present there are between 35 and 40 serving the Lord in many areas. (Approximately the same number are serving churches in Canada and the States.)

"Numbers don't really matter," Paul says, "except as a means of encouragement and challenge. God keeps the books. But it's a real joy to Father—actually, to all of us who have anything to do with the church—to see the interest on the part of young men and women in serving God today."

Sparked by Dr. Smith's use of the faith-promise plan for giving, the missionary offerings have grown from $10,000 the first year to $958,409 in 1975. In 1976, the offering was over $1 million.

And, according to Mr. Whiticar, interest in missions has grown steadily. "The amount of money we have raised has grown in direct proportion to the number of missionaries we have obligated ourselves to support," he continues. "It seems that God has been faithful to send in the funds in relationship to our own faith in Him. I have heard both Drs. Smith say that many times."

The guideline for accepting missionaries for support is almost the same today as it was when the first five missionaries went to the field. They support only those who will be serving with faith missions. "We've felt any denomination that sends out people is obligated to support them and should not have to depend on outside help."

Their attitude toward missionaries from the States is the same. American Christians should support their own missionaries, they feel, and Canadians should assume the responsibility for those from their own country.

"As far as I know," Dr. Paul Smith says, "We have never turned down a Canadian missionary who has been accepted by a recognized faith mission—if we have sufficient funds. We give each missionary we accept $960 a year. If he is from our church the amount is doubled. We do not give toward transportation or equipment costs and we have not supported the children of missionaries up to this point.

"We have no particular reason for limiting our support the way we do. We are well aware that transportation and equipment are important and that children must be supported if their parents are to remain on the field. But we can't do everything. If we pick up support, others will take care of the additional expenses."

There has been one change in recent years. In the beginning nationals were not supported. Now, however, because of the increasing tide of nationalism and the suspicion and distrust aimed at foreigners in so many developing countries, the effectiveness of North American missionaries is severely limited.

"If the work is to be done in some of these countries," Paul Smith observes, "a national has to do it. And if he is to work full time for the Lord, the chances are that he will have to be supported from abroad. The believers in many countries simply don't have the funds available to do so. Father wasn't too keen on it at first, but now he sees the wisdom of the change.''

Dr. Oswald Smith leans back in his chair and his eyes gleam as he recalls the first missionary conference, or convention as he calls it. It was in the heart of the Depression when many were out of work. They could hold three services a day and get people out to them.

"On Sunday we had four meetings," he remembers, "and we were always crowded out. Then times began to get better and men were working again so we cut down to two meetings a day, and finally to one service in the evening.

"Our format for our conventions, or conferences as Paul insists on calling them now, has changed some over the years, but it is still quite recognizable. We always get someone like Dr. Clyde Taylor or Dr. Isaac Paige or some other outstanding authority on the subject of world missions and use him as our main speaker. Even back in those days we saw that we had to have someone who was known well enough so people would want to hear him. He would give the main address of the evening.

"But we did not want the contact of our people with missions to end there. We knew they had to hear missionaries who were actually on the field if their hearts were to burn with the burden for the lost. At those first conventions we had three missionaries from three different fields with us. They spoke two or three minutes each evening and someone showed missionary slides or a 16mm movie taken on the field. We had the speaking, the testimonies of those in active work on the field, and the pictures. Our people learned about missions first and began to get excited about having a part in the ministry in foreign lands.''

The Faith-promise

"We also introduced the faith-promise plan of giving," Oswald Smith continues. "I actually picked up the idea from Dr. A. B. Simpson, founder of the Christian and Missionary Alliance. Only I didn't like calling it a pledge. That sounded too formal and legal to me. What we decided we wanted from our people was a promise to trust God to give them a certain amount of money for foreign missions. It was to be between the individual believer and God. I didn't see the church treasurer even contacting the person to see if he was going to pay the amount. He was promising God. He wasn't promising us."

The results were spectacular and gratifying as the church regularly gave five times as much for missions as they did to support the local church and its activities. With the expanded work and the increased demands for staff and facilities, it has no longer been possible to maintain that ratio, but they do give a dollar for foreign missions to every dollar spent at home. By September 1, 1975 $988,000 had been given for missions since January with more flowing in every Sunday.

"The amount of money that comes in is wonderful." Dr. Paul Smith says. "And I would not want to minimize it. But the biggest gain, I am convinced, is what sacrificial giving can do for the individual spiritually."

A young person associated with the church is an example. His first introduction to giving, strangely enough, was not to missions. The church was moving to Sheppard Avenue, and he felt led to close out his bank account to give the money toward a new pew in the church. When the teller saw his check going through she came to the elevator and begged him to put a stop order on it and use the money as a down payment on a car, instead. But he did not allow her to talk him out of it.

"Even with that gesture I wasn't giving very much or very consistently." he says. "And the increases in my paycheck scarcely kept up the rate of inflation.

"In 1967, shortly after marrying a lovely Christian girl, I decided (with her help) to give on a regular basis and opened a special bank account for that purpose. Over a period of eight years my earnings doubled every three years. The Lord made it possible for me to complete a university program by evening study that has led to a professional accounting degree and has greatly increased my earning capacity.

"He provided us a home at a time when the prices of property in Toronto were out of reach for the average young married couple. Now He has given me a position with a Christian firm.

"And our giving? It has increased from almost $338 in 1967 to over $4,160 in 1974. Approximately three-fourths of our contributions have been to The Peoples Church. The remainder goes to providing Bibles behind the Iron Curtain, supporting regular radio programs to some 20 million Red Chinese, looking after a little girl in Korea, and providing support for less fortunate persons than ourselves.

"It is indeed far more blessed to give than it is to receive. What we have given to God so far cannot possibly cover just the smallest blessing we received from Him during these last seven years."

Conferences

The missionary conference has always been the heart of the emphasis on missions at The Peoples Church. "We begin to prepare for it at least a year in advance," the pastor says, "and we urge our people to keep their own calendars clear for that period of two weeks. We ask the businessmen to plan their out-of-town trips either before or after the conference, if possible. Those who vacation in the spring are expected to avoid being away during our April missionary conference. No other activities are planned by our day school or any other department of the church for those two weeks.

"We discovered a long while ago that people will not place any more importance on an event than the sponsoring organization places on it. And this is important. It is all-important to everyone who is vitally concerned with The Peoples Church and our ministry around the world."

The World Missions Conference still brings in an outstanding North American missionary statesman such as G. Christian Weiss of Back to the Bible Broadcast or Harold Ockenga, former pastor of Boston's Park Street Church, another missions-minded church. The speaker usually stresses the biblical basis for missions, and why we are concerned about those who have never heard the Gospel of Jesus Christ.

Because of the changing face of missions in the modern world with the strong emphasis on nationalism, 10 or 12 national Christian leaders are flown in from all over the world. In 1975 Gus Marwieh and James Kumeh came to tell the people about the spiritual needs as they saw them in Liberia. Moses Ariye represented the believers in Nigeria and shared his burden for the vast numbers who were far from Christ. There was Virgil Zapeta from Guatemala, John Kao of Hong Kong, Enrique Capeda from Mexico, and several others.

The 1975 conference featured men in executive positions and places of authority from many faith missions. Men like Cameron Townsend, Peter Dyneka, Paul C. Dauffman, Everett S. Graffam, and others. This, too, is a regular event for the yearly missions conference.

Another important part of the conference is the appearance of as many missionaries home on furlough as it is possible for the church to get. "From 125 to 175 will be with us any given year," a spokesman for the church says. "And this is a very important part of the conference. If people are going to be concerned about missions they are going to have to learn about them. More important, they are going to have to get acquainted with the missionaries on a personal basis. If you've had a missionary in your home your prayers for him and his family take on a new dimension. You are no longer talking with God about a name. You are interceding with Him for a person—a friend. And when you give, it is the same."

"If we were to stop at this point in our planning we would have a series of meetings that would be unbelievably dull to all but the most dedicated," Pastor Smith says. "And I'm sure our attendance would begin to go down. So we round out our services by bringing in a couple of lively singing groups, one for each of the two weeks. Last year we had the world-traveling Samuelson brothers and the widely known Antone Indian family with us. Their music was a big help in breaking the serious tone of a succession of meetings that could have become boring."

Though the main thrust of the conference is to challenge believers to make faith-promises for world missions, The Peoples Church is also deeply concerned about challenging youth for serving Christ on the mission fields.

Youth Banquets

The day school has a procession of missionaries and nationals speaking to them at chapel during the two-week conference, and effort is made to get the youth out to as many meetings as possible. And on the final Saturday night there is a special banquet just for them. The Youth Interaction Banquet is always held at a nice hotel. In order to keep the price of the ticket down to a point where the teenagers and young adults in the church will feel they can afford to go, the banquet is subsidized.

In 1975 it was held at the Four Seasons-Sheraton Hotel with 1,780 in attendance. A missionary sat at each table with eight or ten kids.

As the host of his table, he had the opportunity to get personally acquainted with those who were seated with him.

"We have two purposes for the youth banquet," Paul Smith says. "First, we are anxious to present missions and to challenge our Christian young people with the importance of spreading the Gospel of Jesus Christ around the world. I am convinced in the five years that we have had these banquets a significant number of kids have begun to prepare for the mission field because of what they heard and saw there.

"Second, we want to demonstrate the importance of missions by making this banquet the high point, socially, in our youth church activities. A lot of our kids tell us that the banquet is the major social event in their lives each year.

"Too many people think of missions and missionary effort in the church as a group of women getting together to make bandages. We want to show our youth that missions are important. I believe we can do this by the importance we place on them."

In 1976 the banquet was limited to 1,000. "We would have liked to have had a group as large as the one we had in 1975," one of the staff explained, "but we all felt that the crowd was so big it was unwieldy and too impersonal."

On Sunday the emphasis is on the faith-promise program. It begins with the Sunday School service and goes on through the morning and evening meetings.

Over $400,000 was raised through the Sunday School in 1975.

The faith-promise envelopes are used in the primary classes and up.

"We are not thinking about money so far as the children are concerned," according to the pastor. "If we were, we would not have the lower grades take part in the program. In some cases we don't even get enough from them to pay for the material used. But we are striving to teach them to have a concern and compassion for those who have never had a chance to know about Jesus Christ.

"We had an article in our magazine not long ago about a member of our church who came over from Germany as a young man. He said he had been taught to believe that if God wanted money for His work He would bring about a miracle. As a result the young man never learned to give.

"We know that God has chosen to work through us, and, in a way, to limit Himself to our devotion to Him and our willingness to share what He has given us. This is the message we are trying to get across to our kids. We want them to know that they have a responsibility to give. We want to teach them the joy of sharing.

"Most of the missionary giving is promised during the conference. No particular stress is placed on cash gifts at that time but a sizeable amount of cash comes in."

One of the long-time members of the church remembers raising money to pay her faith-promise when she was a little girl. It was during the depression and cash was hard to come by. There were few jobs, even for adults, and an allowance for a child was almost unheard of.

A man traveled up and down the streets in the section of Toronto where she lived with her parents, using his horse-drawn wagon to transport the old rags and bottles he bought. She gathered up enough of those items and sold them to pay her promise to the missions program.

"I think I learned more about giving through that experience than in anything I ever did," she says, "and I developed a love for missions that is still with me."

"Not everyone who makes a faith-promise keeps it," Paul volunteered. "I suppose some lose interest. Some feel because of illness or financial reverses that they simply cannot keep it, and some get caught in the spiral of ever-rising prices which makes it difficult for them to give as much as they thought they could.

"It is surprising, however, to see how many do give what they have promised. And for everyone who fails to honor his promised gift it seems that there are one or two who do far more than they ever thought they could. As a result we always go over the amount we have pledged."

For The Peoples Church the World Missions Conference has proved to be a most effective means of keeping the needs of missions and missionaries before their people. And it has helped challenge their youth for full-time Christian service as well.

"I would not even try to pastor a church without a missions conference of some sort," Dr. Paul Smith observes. "It has been the very heart of that phase of our ministry."

10

Telethons

In 1975 a new dimension was added to the World Missions Conference in the form of a two-hour telethon or television special on the middle Sunday of the two-week conference. The church bought time on six or eight Ontario TV stations for the purpose of raising money for the World Relief Commission of the National Association of Evangelicals to use in their emergency program in the south Sahara. The need was presented and a group of volunteers manned a bank of telephones to take the calls of those who wished to contribute.

The idea was not original with The Peoples Church. It has long been used by such organizations as the Canadian Cancer Society and the Heart Fund. At least one faith literature mission has adopted that method to help them raise funds for their ministry. They have had varying degrees of success in different parts of the country.

"We evangelicals have often been accused of being unconcerned about the physical needs of people in other lands," Paul Smith points out, turning his attention to the TV special. "I've visited mission fields all over the world and so has my father. We know from what we have seen that the charges laid against us by liberals are unjust.

"Almost every leprosarium in the entire world has its roots in evangelical Christianity. They were all organized and operated by true believers. And wherever missionaries have gone they have built schools and hospitals and have trained people to man them. You will even find evangelical agricultural experts in the fields around the world teaching nationals how to do a better job of feeding their own people by raising better crops.

"We have been deeply concerned about the increasing physical needs of the people in the drought-stricken sections of Africa, and the need for food, clothing, and medicine in much of India, Bangladesh, Indonesia, and elsewhere. So we decided that the TV special was to be for raising funds for the south Sahara, one of the most needy areas in all the world. We figured it would accomplish two purposes. It would raise funds for world relief and would also dramatize to Toronto and our part of Ontario that the Christian does care about the physical needs of those who are less fortunate than himself.

"We had no idea what to expect in the way of returns, but the television people thought we might be able to raise as much as $50,000 if the appeal was well handled and the program professionally done. They were basing their estimate on their experience with other charitable organizations in similar television campaigns."

The task of working out the multitude of details and setting up the telethon was shared by the entire church staff. Much had to be done before the special program was aired. A format had to be worked out, personnel had to be recruited and trained, and the telephones and special lines that were needed had to be arranged for.

"We had a bank of nine phones set up in Founders Hall," Mr. Whiticar explains. "We used three phones in the church and two in the school, making a total of fourteen."

Forty-seven girls volunteered to help with taking the calls as they came in. They had to be trained to answer the calls quickly and courteously, get all the pertinent information, and free the line as quickly as possible. They had to learn how to get rid of the inevitable crank callers."

The smaller gifts were accepted without verification but every gift that would total more than $500 for the year was verified with a phone call.

"We didn't take their numbers when they phoned in their faith-promises," Mr. Whiticar says. "This was deliberate. We looked up their numbers in the phone book and got back to them later. If we weren't able to get to them, the amount wasn't counted into the total figure.

"There were some calls we didn't get verified until well into the following week, but, surprisingly, there were few that were thrown out. Most of the calls were genuine."

The theme of the special was "Survival or Starvation?" "You should have seen some of the slides we used," Dr. Paul Smith comments. "They were graphic. Starvation is a terrible thing and those of us who live in our tight little North American world don't really know what it is not to have enough food. The pictures showing starvation are guaranteed to destroy the complacency of any thinking Christian."

They raised a total of $169,000. Some of the promises did not materialize but enough additional money came in to more than make up for those promises that were not honored.

There were some unusual calls. One Jewish woman was noticeably irritated when she phoned an hour or so after the church went off the air. "What are you doing down there at The Peoples Church, anyway?" she demanded.

The girl told her.

"My number is just one digit different from yours," she complained, "and my phone's been ringing off the wall."

"We're sorry you've been inconvenienced," the girl from the church told her, "but we're doing this TV special to raise money for the people in the south Sahara who are starving."

"Well, I don't like the way the phone's been bothering me," the caller continued, "but I've raised money for the Canadian Cancer Society and Mt. Sinai Hospital and several other organizations. Get your pencil and paper. I've taken down these faith-promises for you."

Though the program went off the air at 1 o'clock, it was 5:40 p.m. before the girls could be relieved to go to dinner. In spite of the hectic afternoon most of the volunteers were thrilled at having had a part in it.

"I was exhausted when we got through," one said, "but it was a tremendous experience."

The television special was so successful the staff started planning almost immediately for the next year's special. They went over it carefully, trying to analyze what they did and to see if there were better, more efficient methods. "Probably we will refine the mechanics," Paul said, "but the biggest change will come in the phoning from out-of-Toronto places like Owen Sound, Ottawa, Sudbury, etc. Arrangements will be made for some phones so there will be less congestion of the lines at the church and to cut down on the cost by eliminating the need for using long distance in making promises."

Missions-minded

Though the main missionary thrust at The Peoples Church is during the conference, there is a strong missionary emphasis all year.

"I think this is one of the problems some churches have in attempting to make their people missions-minded," Paul Smith says. "They will have some sort of special thrust for a few days and get a little momentum. Then they will decide they have done their duty toward missions for another year and sit back until all the interest has been dissipated. You've got to keep everlastingly at it if you want the people in your church to be missionary-minded."

Since the day school came into being missionary speakers have been used there at every opportunity, according to Dr. Edmundson, Minister of Education. The same is true of the regular services at church.

"We may only be able to spare a missionary or the representative from a faith mission for three to five minutes," a staff member says, "but we always try to work them into our services. When we do, we are accomplishing two things. We're providing a missionary speaker with a platform to present his particular area of service, but I believe the other thing we accomplish is even more important. When we give a missionary time in our service, this is what we're telling the church: 'Look, it's important for you to know about missions. It's so important we're re-arranging our program to allow a missionary to tell us what he is doing.' "

But this isn't all. The church distributes a quarterly magazine which publicizes what is going on in all avenues of the ministry, but particularly in the field of missions. There are stories about the blessings of giving to foreign fields, the accounts of individual missionaries and articles that deal with the trends in missions around the world.

"We want our people to be well informed," according to the pastor. "That is one of the precepts Father always worked on. He felt that people could not know how to give or pray intelligently unless they were aware of what was going on. I think this has been one of the prime reasons for his traveling overseas. He actually made himself an authority on missions so he could relay accurate information to our people.

"When a change in the political situation in a given country may affect the work of the Lord, we want our people to know about it. Our magazine is not the only means we use for that purpose. I suppose the pulpit is more often the means by which our people learn what is currently going on in missions, but the magazine is important. Without it I'm sure our evangelical thrust overseas would not be nearly as effective."

Another important factor is the "bookstore." Paul Smith looks back to his father's books and the fact that a book played such a large part in his father's interest in missions and missionaries. If books could work in one individual's life, he reasoned, they could work in the hearts of many.

"We have the book tables because of the blessing books can be to our people," the senior pastor went on. "Who knows? Perhaps another David Brainard or a Hudson Taylor is going to church here right now. Maybe God is trying to work in the heart of some lad who can pick up a missionary book from our racks, or the story of Father's life as a boy and be profoundly affected by it. Perhaps a book is just what is needed to get his feet on the right track and keep them there.

"Perhaps a bewildered young woman has been weighing her

commitment to the mission field against her love for a boy who is indifferent to serving Jesus Christ. We have had young people come to us with the story that at a critical time in their spiritual lives God has used a book to guide them.

"We've seen these things happen with Father's books and with my own. This is the reason we have books for sale. They are available on Sunday because that is when the people are around."

The book tables have a representative stock of evangelical books and records, including Dr. Oswald Smith's many volumes and those written by Paul. There are Bibles, a selection of missionary biographies, a few kids' books, and some records and tapes.

What makes the missionary program at The Peoples Church effective? It's the constant emphasis on missions, missionaries, and their activities. There's the magazine, the book tables, the World Missions Conference, and the Faith-promise plan for raising funds. Perhaps the most important factor, however, is the Women's Prayer Group. They not only pray for the general needs of the work including those who are ill, but once a month they have a day of prayer, during which they divide into pairs and pray for the missionaries by name and by need. None of the 465 workers around the world is forgotten in these prayer meetings.

11

Sage Advice

Dr. Paul Smith leaned back in his chair and clasped his hands behind his head, closing his eyes for a time.

"What advice would I give a pastor who wants to challenge his church to be evangelistic and to have a vigorous missionary program? To begin with I would tell him not to copy exactly what we do. Our methods are successful here but they may not work for him and his people.

"Let me explain. As everyone knows, Jack Hyles has a tremendous church with an outreach unequaled anywhere in the States or Canada. A lot of men, and particularly young men, will see what is happening as a result of Hyles' busing program and will rush to Hammond to find out how he does it.

"They come home excited about what they have seen and are sure that all they have to do is to get a certain number of buses and they will soon have a church the equal of Hyles'. All too often something goes wrong and they are bitterly disappointed.

"There is much that can be learned from a church like Hyles', but we must constantly be aware of the fact that God led Hyles to the sort of program that suited his personality, the personality of the people he is reaching, and the type of area he is working in. What he does may or may not be right for a different situation with different people and a pastor with a different personality.

"The same is true if one were to consider modeling another church program after the things we are doing. We may have methods another pastor could adapt to his situation but he should not follow our methods, or those of anyone else, exactly.

"I am not certain that methods are even the important factors some would make them today. There are churches that have been completely revitalized by using the Kennedy plan of visitation. We have tried various visitation programs and have fallen flat on our faces every time.

"I do believe, however, that certain guidelines have been developed through the years at The Peoples Church which can be helpful to any pastor or congregation.

"We have had a singleness of purpose all these years; that of reaching the lost for Christ, both abroad and at home. We have had a love for people and a deep concern for souls.

"Love doesn't just happen, like the measles, or freckles on a nose. Love has to be preached and demonstrated. People have to see love on the part of the pastor before they can have love for each other and for the lost.

"The pastor must also place a high priority on souls. Father used to tell me that we could never expect our people to be more concerned about souls than we were, as pastors. If people see us agonizing over the lost they will have more of a burden themselves.

"And, regardless of whether a church uses visitation like the Coral Ridge Presbyterian Church in Florida, a host of outstations like the Highland Park Baptist Church in Chattanooga, Tennessee, or evangelistic meetings like we do, the Christians must have a burden and be praying or the program will be worthless.

"Then the members of the congregation must know how to present Christ, on a personal basis, to the uncommitted. One of Dr. D'Sena's chief responsibilities is to train counselors for our many campaigns and special meetings. He teaches the concerned believer how to open his Bible and show someone else how the Word of God can change his life by outlining the way of salvation to him.

"The next step is to have an adequate follow-up program. It is not enough to lead an individual to Christ. He has to be taught carefully, step by step. Some have been able to do a good job by having a special class for new believers but that has never worked well for us. Most of the converts who make The Peoples Church their church home want to be a part of a group that includes their friends and acquaintances.

"We have found that a personal contact by a fellow believer, designed to get the new Christian active in Sunday School and church is one of the most effective methods of follow up for us. The method doesn't really matter, but special attention has to be given to new believers.

"The pastor must also show his own concern for missions by the importance he places on missionary work. If missions are accorded a high priority on the church calendar, if the pastor frequently shows missionary films, if he takes every opportunity to have qualified missionary speakers in the pulpit, the people are going to develop an interest in missions.

"Equally important is giving the people an opportunity to get to know missionaries on a personal basis, to have them in their homes and to learn their problems and joys and prayer needs. I even think it helps to let people know the missionaries' short-comings. They will begin to see missionaries as people who need prayer. I'm afraid too many believers have the idea that a missionary is some sort of super-Christian who is far above the problems and realities of life. If people learn to know a person, they they can pray for him or her far more effectively.

"I think this is particularly true of young people. I've been interested in watching the homes that have had close contact with missions and missionaries when the children were growing up. I don't have statistics to prove this, but my observation leads me to believe that a far higher percentage of such children become missionaries themselves. They learn what it's all about, and God uses that to touch their hearts and make them want to serve him.

"Young people need to be challenged in other ways by the needs of missionaries. A smaller church would not be able to have a Youth Interaction Banquet with 1,780 in attendance, but they might be able to do it on a smaller scale. Or they could have fellowship in a number of homes while having visiting missionaries.

A missionary meeting with five or six kids can have a tremendous impact on them. They can ask questions they might be reluctant to ask in a large meeting. A missionary might feel much more free to answer half a dozen kids frankly than he would a group of 500 or 1,500.

"It can be a big help in encouraging missions to get kids active in some sort of Christian outreach. Churches of all sizes have sent kids into home mission situations with the American or Canadian Indians or in a minority group in the inner city. They have repaired churches and homes, helped take care of babies, and taught Vacation Bible School. Again I don't have figures to substantiate this, but I am confident that such types of service result in many, many young men and women going into full-time missionary service.

"The faith-promise plan is an exception to everything I have said about not adapting programs in their entirety from other churches. This in one plan that will work anywhere, in any type of situation, with any people. And any pastor can use it, effectively.

"It is so simple there scarcely needs to be any explanation of how to go about it. Missions and the needs of missions are presented as forcefully as possible. Then cards are handed out and the people are encouraged to promise how much they will give, by faith, to support missions for each month during the coming year. It is not a pledge. The individual is not contacted and asked to pay. It is a promise to God that he will keep if God provides him with the means. He is trusting God to provide this gift of love.

"We start with the primary kids and begin to teach them the blessing of giving regularly so that others might hear the good news of salvation. Over the years we have seen how effective this is in teaching a deep love and concern for the lost.

"I have seen many churches adopt this plan and Father has seen far more because he has pushed it harder than I have. We know from the results that the faith-promise plan will increase the giving for missions dramatically."

Dr. Paul Smith's Suggestions
for Revitalizing Your Church

EVANGELISM
1. The people must have a love for unbelievers.
2. They must have a deep concern for souls.
3. There must be a high priority on soul-winning and evangelism.
4. There must be consistent prayer for the lost.
5. The congregation must be taught to present Christ to the seeking.
6. There must be an adequate follow-up program.

MISSIONS
1. The people must have the same love and concern for those who live in pagan cultures that they have for their Christian friends.
2. They must place a high priority on missions in their attitude and on the church calendar.
3. They must have the opportunity to know missionaries personally.
4. They must learn to pray intelligently for missions and missionaries.
5. Youth must be challenged by the needs of missions and those serving abroad.
6. The faith-promise type of giving should be adopted. It can greatly increase the financial outreach of any congregation and never hurts the local budget if it is done right.

Inspirational Victor Books for Your Enjoyment

HOW GOD CAN USE NOBODIES A study, by James Montgomery Boice, of the lives of Abraham, Moses, and David—Old Testament men who were small enough to be great. Textbook **6-2027—$1.75**/Leader's Guide **6-2922—95¢**

THE BEGINNING A study of Genesis by Les Woodson. Treats Genesis as the beginning of God's everlasting righteous kingdom. Textbook **6-2713—$1.95**/Leader's Guide **6-2916—95¢**

WHAT WORKS WHEN LIFE DOESN'T? What works when happiness eludes you? You face discouragement? In 12 selected Psalms, Stuart Briscoe stays close to the biblical text, yet uses contemporary anecdotes and relevant applications for a very practical study that answers these questions and more. Text book **6-2725—$1.95**/Leader's Guide (with transparency masters) **6-2946—$1.95**

BE FREE An expository study of Galatians by Warren W. Wiersbe. Challenges the Christian to recognize and live according to the true freedom he has in Christ. Leader's Guide includes overhead projector masters, with instructions for making transparencies. Textbook **6-2716—$1.75**/Leader's Guide **6-2938—$1.95**

KNOW THE MARKS OF CULTS Dave Breese exposes common and characteristic errors of all cults. Sounds a warning and a note of encouragement to true believers. Textbook **6-2704—$1.50**/Leader's Guide **6-2917—95¢**

THE FRAGRANCE OF BEAUTY Scripturally based study, by Joyce Landorf, on wrong attitudes that mar a woman's beauty—and help for correcting them. Textbook **6-2231—$1.50**/Leader's Guide **6-2912—95¢**

24 WAYS TO IMPROVE YOUR TEACHING Dr. Kenneth Gangel, experienced Christian educator, describes 24 teaching methods, and gives concrete suggestions for using them in teaching the Word of God. Leader's Guide includes overhead projector masters, with instructions for making transparencies. Textbook **6-2463—$1.95**/Leader's Guide **6-2927—$1.95**

THE COMPLETE CHRISTIAN Larry Richards gives insights for life from the Book of Hebrews. Emphasizes reaching spiritual maturity thru steady growth and faith. Leader's Guide includes overhead projector masters, with instructions for making transparencies. Textbook **6-2714—$1.75**/Leader's Guide **6-2937—$1.95**

WHAT HAPPENS WHEN WOMEN PRAY Evelyn Christenson, with Viola Blake, deals with methods and spiritual principles of prayer. Inspirational and practical. Textbook **6-2715—$1.75**/Leader's Guide **6-2943—95¢**

DISCIPLES ARE MADE—NOT BORN Walt Henrichsen, personnel director worldwide for The Navigators, discusses what discipleship is and the training of a disciple. Textbook **6-2706—$1.75**/Leader's Guide **6-2919—95¢**

̶d 40¢ postage and handling for the first book, and 10¢ ̶h additional title. Add $1 for minimum order service ̶ orders less than $5.

̶OR BOOKS

a division of SP Publications, Inc.
WHEATON, ILLINOIS 60187